I0011685

Murat Durmus

A Hands-On Introduction to
**Essential Python
Libraries and Frameworks**

(With Code Samples)

Copyright © 2023 Murat Durmus

All rights reserved. No part of this publication may be reproduced, distributed, or transmitted in any form or by any means, including photocopying, recording, or other electronic or mechanical methods, without the prior written permission of the publisher, except in the case of brief quotations embodied in critical reviews and certain other noncommercial uses permitted by copyright law.

Cover design:

Murat Durmus

About the Author

Murat Durmus is CEO and founder of AISOMA (a Frankfurt am Main (Germany) based company specializing in AI-based technology development and consulting) and Author of the books "Mindful AI - Reflections on Artificial Intelligence".& "A Primer to the 42 Most commonly used Machine Learning Algorithms (With Code Samples)"

You can get in touch with the author via:

- LinkedIn: https://www.linkedin.com/in/ceosaisoma/

- E-Mail: murat.durmus@aisoma.de

Note:

The code examples and their description in this book were written with the support of ChatGPT (OpenAI).

"Python is not just a language, it's a community where developers can learn, collaborate and create wonders."

- Guido van Rossum

(Creator of Python)

A BRIEF HISTORY OF PYTHON PROGRAMMING LANGUAGE

Python is a popular high-level programming language for various applications, including web development, scientific computing, data analysis, and machine learning. Its simplicity, readability, and versatility have made it a popular choice for programmers of all levels of expertise. Here is a brief history of Python programming language.

Python was created in the late 1980s by Guido van Rossum, who worked at the National Research Institute for Mathematics and Computer Science in the Netherlands. Van Rossum was looking for a programming language that was easy to read and write, and that could be used for various applications. He named the language after the British comedy group Monty Python, as he was a fan of their TV show.

The first version of Python, Python 0.9.0, was released in 1991. This version included many features still used in PythonPython today, such as modules, exceptions, and the core data types of lists, dictionaries, and tuples.

Python 1.0 was released in 1994 and included many new features, such as lambda, map, filter, and reduce. These features made it easier to write functional-style code in PythonPython.

Python 2.0 was released in 2000, introducing list comprehensions, a new garbage collector, and a cycle-detecting garbage collector. List comprehensions made writing code that operated on lists and other iterable objects easier.

Python 3.0, a significant update to the language, was released in 2008. This version introduced many changes and improvements, including a redesigned print function, new string formatting syntax, and a new division operator. The latest version also removed some features that were considered outdated or redundant.

Since the release of Python 3.0, there have been several minor releases, each introducing new features and improvements while maintaining backward compatibility with existing code. These releases have included features such as async/await syntax for asynchronous programming, type annotations for improved code readability and maintainability, and improvements to the garbage collector and the standard library.

Python's popularity has grown steadily over the years, and it is now one of the most popular programming languages in the world. Web developers, data scientists, and machine learning engineers, among others, widely use it. Python's popularity has been driven by its simplicity, readability, and versatility, as well as its large and active community of developers who contribute to the language and its ecosystem of libraries and tools.

In conclusion, Python programming language has come a long way since its inception in the late 1980s. It has undergone many changes and improvements over the years, but its core values of simplicity, readability, and versatility have remained constant. Moreover, Python's popularity shows no signs of slowing down, and it will likely remain a popular choice for programmers for many years.

At a glance:

- Python was created by Guido van Rossum in the late 1980s while he was working at the National Research Institute for Mathematics and Computer Science in the Netherlands.

- The first version of Python, Python 0.9.0, was released in 1991.

- Python 1.0 was released in 1994, which included many new features such as lambda, map, filter, and reduce.

- Python 2.0 was released in 2000, which introduced list comprehensions, a new garbage collector, and a cycle-detecting garbage collector.

- Python 3.0, a major update to the language, was released in 2008. This version introduced many changes and improvements, including a redesigned print function, new string formatting syntax, and a new division operator.

- Since the release of Python 3.0, there have been several minor releases, each introducing new features and improvements while maintaining backwards compatibility with existing code.

- Python has become one of the most popular programming languages in the world, used for a wide variety of applications such as web development, scientific computing, data analysis, and machine learning.

- **Python's popularity has been driven by its simplicity, readability, and versatility, as well as its large and active community of developers who contribute to the language and its ecosystem of libraries and tools.**

DATA SCIENCE

Data science is an interdisciplinary field that involves extracting, analyzing, and interpreting large, complex data sets. It combines elements of statistics, computer science, and domain expertise to extract insights and knowledge from data.

Data scientists use various tools and techniques to collect, process, and analyze data, including statistical analysis, machine learning, data mining, and data visualization. They work with large, complex data sets to uncover patterns, relationships, and insights that can inform decision-making and drive business value.

Data science has applications in various fields, including business, healthcare, finance, and social science. It informs different decisions, from product development to marketing to policy-making.

PANDAS

Python Pandas is an open-source data manipulation and analysis library for the Python programming language. It provides a set of data structures for efficiently storing and manipulating large data sets, as well as a variety of tools for data analysis, cleaning, and preprocessing.

Some of the key data structures in Pandas include the Series, which is a one-dimensional array-like object that can hold any data type; and the DataFrame, which is a two-dimensional tabular data structure with rows and columns that can be thought of as a spreadsheet or a SQL table.

Pandas also provides a range of data manipulation functions and methods, such as filtering, sorting, merging, grouping, and aggregating data. It also supports data visualization tools that allow users to plot and visualize data in a variety of ways.

It is widely used in data analysis and data science, and is considered one of the essential tools for working with data in Python. It is also frequently used in conjunction with other popular data science libraries such as NumPy, Matplotlib, and SciPy.

An example of how you can use Pandas to read in a CSV file, manipulate the data, and then output it to a new file:

```python
import pandas as pd

# Read in the CSV file
data = pd.read_csv('my_data.csv')

# Print the first few rows of the data
```

```
print(data.head())

# Filter the data to include only rows where
the 'score' column is greater than 90
filtered_data = data[data['score'] > 90]

# Create a new column that calculates the
average of the 'score' and 'time' columns
filtered_data['average'] =
(filtered_data['score'] +
filtered_data['time']) / 2

# Output the filtered data to a new CSV file
filtered_data.to_csv('my_filtered_data.csv',
index=False)
```

In this example, we first import the Pandas library using **import pandas as pd**. We then read in a CSV file called **my_data.csv** using the **pd.read_csv()** function, which creates a DataFrame object. We then use the **head()** method to print out the first few rows of the data.

Next, we filter the data to include only rows where the 'score' column is greater than 90 using boolean indexing. We then create a new column called 'average' that calculates the average of the 'score' and 'time' columns using basic arithmetic operations.

Finally, we use the **to_csv()** method to output the filtered data to a new CSV file called **my_filtered_data.csv**, with the **index=False** parameter indicating that we do not want to include the DataFrame index as a column in the output file.

7

Pros and Cons

Pros:

- Easy-to-use and highly versatile library for data manipulation and analysis.

- Provides powerful tools for handling large datasets, including fast indexing, filtering, grouping, and merging operations.

- Supports a wide range of input and output formats, including CSV, Excel, SQL databases, and JSON.

- Offers a rich set of data visualization tools, including line plots, scatter plots, histograms, and more.

- Has a large and active community of users and developers, which means that there is a wealth of online resources and support available.

- Can be used in conjunction with other popular data science libraries such as NumPy, SciPy, and Matplotlib.

Cons:

- Pandas can be memory-intensive when working with very large datasets, and may not be the best choice for real-time applications or very high-dimensional data.

- Some of the functions and methods can be complex and difficult to understand, especially for new users.

- Can be slow when performing certain operations, such as applying functions to large datasets or performing multiple merges or concatenations.

- May not always produce the desired results, especially when working with messy or unstructured data.

- Some users have reported issues with compatibility and portability between different versions of Pandas or between Pandas and other libraries.

NUMPY

NumPy is a Python library for numerical computing. It provides powerful data structures, such as n-dimensional arrays or "ndarrays", and a wide range of mathematical functions for working with these arrays efficiently.

It is widely used in data science, machine learning, scientific computing, and engineering, among other fields. It is built on top of low-level languages like C and Fortran, which allows NumPy to be fast and efficient even when working with large datasets.

In addition to its core functionality, NumPy also provides tools for integrating with other scientific computing libraries in Python, such as SciPy and Pandas. Overall, NumPy is an essential tool for anyone working with numerical data in Python.

An example code that demonstrates how to create a NumPy array, perform mathematical operations on it, and slice it:

```python
import numpy as np

# Create a 1-dimensional NumPy array
arr = np.array([1, 2, 3, 4, 5])

# Perform mathematical operations on the array
print("Original array:", arr)
print("Array multiplied by 2:", arr * 2)
print("Array squared:", arr ** 2)
print("Array sine values:", np.sin(arr))

# Create a 2-dimensional NumPy array
```

```
arr2d = np.array([[1, 2, 3], [4, 5, 6], [7, 8,
9]])

# Slice the array to get a subarray
sub_arr = arr2d[:2, 1:]
print("Original 2D array:\n", arr2d)
print("Subarray:\n", sub_arr)
```

Output:

```
Original array: [1 2 3 4 5]
Array multiplied by 2: [ 2   4   6   8 10]
Array squared: [ 1   4   9 16 25]
Array sine values: [ 0.84147098  0.90929743
0.14112001 -0.7568025  -0.95892427]
Original 2D array:
 [[1 2 3]
 [4 5 6]
 [7 8 9]]
Subarray:
 [[2 3]
 [5 6]]
```

In this example, we import the NumPy library and create a one-dimensional array **arr** with the values **[1, 2, 3, 4, 5]**. We then perform several mathematical operations on the array, such as multiplication by 2 and squaring the values, using NumPy functions.

Next, we create a two-dimensional array **arr2d** with the values **[[1, 2, 3], [4, 5, 6], [7, 8, 9]]**. We slice this array to get a subarray **sub_arr** containing the elements in the first two rows and the last two columns. We print the original arrays and the subarray to show the results.

Pros and Cons

Pros:

- Efficient and fast: NumPy is built on top of low-level languages like C and Fortran, which makes it much faster and more efficient than pure Python code for numerical computations.

- Powerful data structures: NumPy provides powerful n-dimensional arrays, or "ndarrays", which allow for efficient storage and manipulation of large datasets.

- Comprehensive mathematical functions: NumPy provides a wide range of mathematical functions, such as trigonometric, logarithmic, and statistical functions, which makes it easy to perform complex computations on arrays.

- Integration with other Python libraries: NumPy integrates seamlessly with other scientific computing libraries in Python, such as SciPy, Pandas, and Matplotlib, which allows for more advanced data analysis and visualization.

Cons:

- Steep learning curve: NumPy can be challenging to learn, especially for beginners who are not familiar with programming concepts like arrays and vectorization.

- Memory usage: NumPy arrays can use a lot of memory, which can be a problem when working with very large datasets.

- Lack of flexibility: NumPy is optimized for numerical computations and is not as flexible as pure Python code for general-purpose programming tasks.

Overall, the pros of NumPy far outweigh the cons, especially when working with large datasets or performing complex numerical computations. However, it's important to keep the limitations of NumPy in mind and choose the right tool for the job.

SEABORN

Seaborn is a Python data visualization library built on top of Matplotlib. It provides a high-level interface for creating informative and attractive statistical graphics in Python.

It offers a range of visualization techniques for statistical graphics, including:

- **Univariate and bivariate plots**: Histograms, kernel density estimates, box plots, violin plots, and scatter plots.

- **Regression and categorical plots**: Linear regression, logistic regression, categorical scatter plots, and bar plots.

- **Matrix plots**: Heatmaps, cluster maps, and pair plots.

- **Time series plots**: Line plots, time series heatmaps, and seasonal plots.

Seaborn is designed to work seamlessly with Pandas, a popular data manipulation library in Python, and it can handle large and complex datasets with ease. It also provides a range of customization options for plots, including color palettes, themes, and styling.

Overall, Seaborn is a powerful and user-friendly library for creating informative and visually appealing statistical graphics in Python.

An example code using Seaborn to create a scatter plot:

```
import seaborn as sns
import pandas as pd

# Load dataset
df = pd.read_csv('my_dataset.csv')

# Create scatter plot
sns.scatterplot(x='x_column', y='y_column',
data=df)

# Show plot
sns.plt.show()
```

In this example, we first import the Seaborn library and Pandas library for loading and manipulating the dataset. We then load the dataset from a CSV file using Pandas.

Next, we create a scatter plot using Seaborn's **scatterplot()** function, passing the names of the x and y columns from the dataset as arguments. We also pass the **data** argument to specify the dataset we want to plot.

Finally, we use Seaborn's **plt.show()** function to display the plot on the screen. Seaborn automatically styles the plot with an attractive default theme, and we can customize the plot further using other Seaborn functions and arguments.

This code creates a scatter plot that shows the relationship between two variables in the dataset, where the x-axis represents the "x_column" variable and the y-axis represents the "y_column" variable. Each point in the scatter plot represents a single observation in the dataset. Seaborn automatically adds labels to the axes and a legend explaining the meaning of the different colors in the plot.

Pros and Cons

Pros:

- Attractive and informative visualizations: Seaborn provides a range of visualization techniques that are optimized for creating attractive and informative statistical graphics in Python. It offers a wide range of customization options for colors, styles, and themes, which makes it easy to create visually appealing plots that are tailored to the needs of the user.

- User-friendly interface: Seaborn is designed to be easy to use, with a simple and consistent API that makes it easy to create complex visualizations with just a few lines of code. It also provides a range of built-in datasets that can be used for practice or exploration.

- Integration with Pandas: Seaborn is designed to work seamlessly with Pandas, a popular data manipulation library in Python, which makes it easy to handle and visualize large and complex datasets.

- Versatility: Seaborn offers a wide range of visualization techniques, including univariate and bivariate plots, regression and categorical plots, matrix plots, and time series plots, which makes it a versatile tool for data exploration and analysis.

Cons:

- Limited scope: Seaborn is focused on statistical data visualization and is not as flexible as other visualization libraries for general-purpose data visualization tasks.

- Steep learning curve: Although Seaborn is designed to be easy to use, some users may find it challenging to learn, especially if they are not familiar with statistical visualization concepts or the Pandas library.

- Limited customization options: Although Seaborn offers a wide range of customization options, some users may find that they are limited in the level of customization they can achieve, especially compared to more advanced visualization libraries like Matplotlib.

Overall, the pros of Seaborn far outweigh the cons, especially for users who need to create informative and attractive statistical graphics in Python. However, it's important to keep the limitations of Seaborn in mind and choose the right tool for the job.

SCIPY

Scipy is an open-source scientific computing library for Python that provides a collection of functions for mathematics, science, and engineering. It is built on top of the NumPy library, which provides efficient array operations for numerical computing.

It is organized into subpackages that provide different functionalities, such as:

- **Integration and optimization**

- **Signal and image processing**

- **Statistics and probability**

- **Interpolation and extrapolation**

- **Sparse matrix and linear algebra**

- **Special functions and numerical routines**

Scipy is widely used in scientific research, engineering, data science, and other fields where numerical computation is required. It provides a convenient and powerful way to perform complex calculations and analysis in Python, with a large and active community of users and developers who contribute to its development and maintenance.

An example code using Scipy to perform numerical integration:

```python
import numpy as np
from scipy.integrate import quad

# Define function to integrate
def f(x):
    return np.exp(-x ** 2)

# Perform numerical integration
result, error = quad(f, -np.inf, np.inf)

# Print result
print("Result:", result)
print("Error:", error)
```

In this example, we first import the NumPy library and the **quad** function from the Scipy **integrate** subpackage. We then define a function **f(x)** that we want to integrate.

Next, we use the **quad** function to perform numerical integration of **f(x)** over the range from negative infinity to positive infinity. The **quad** function returns the result of the integration and an estimate of the error.

Finally, we print the result and the error to the console. In this case, the result should be the square root of pi (approximately 1.77245385091).

This code demonstrates how Scipy can be used to perform complex mathematical calculations, such as numerical integration, with ease and efficiency in Python.

Pros and Cons

Pros:

- Provides a comprehensive set of tools for scientific computing and numerical analysis, including integration, optimization, signal processing, linear algebra, and more.

- Built on top of NumPy, making it easy to work with arrays and perform efficient numerical operations.

- Large and active community of users and developers, with many open-source packages and modules available for extending its functionality.

- Well-documented with many examples and tutorials available online.

- Portable and cross-platform, supporting many operating systems and hardware architectures.

Cons:

- Can be complex and difficult to learn for beginners due to the many functions and subpackages available.

- Some functions may be computationally intensive and require advanced knowledge of numerical analysis and performance optimization.

- Some functions may have limitations or assumptions that may not be suitable for all applications.

- Requires careful consideration of precision and accuracy in numerical calculations, especially for scientific applications where accuracy is critical.

- Some functions may not be as fast as optimized code written in lower-level languages like C or Fortran.

Overall, Scipy is a powerful and widely-used library for scientific computing in Python, but it may not be the best choice for all applications, and careful consideration of its strengths and limitations is necessary to use it effectively.

MATPLOTLIB

Matplotlib is a popular data visualization library for the Python programming language. It provides a way to create a wide range of static, animated, and interactive visualizations in Python.

It was originally developed by John D. Hunter in 2003 and is now maintained by a team of developers. It is open-source software and is available under a BSD-style license.

Matplotlib is designed to work well with NumPy, a popular numerical computing library for Python, and is often used in conjunction with other scientific computing libraries such as SciPy and Pandas.

It provides a wide range of plotting functionality, including line plots, scatter plots, bar charts, histograms, 3D plots, and more. It also provides a high degree of customization, allowing users to modify almost every aspect of their plots, including the axes, labels, colors, and styles.

It can be used in a variety of settings, from exploratory data analysis to scientific research to creating publication-quality graphics. It is widely used in academia and industry, and is considered one of the essential tools in the Python data science ecosystem.

An example code snippet that uses Matplotlib to create a simple line plot:

```python
import matplotlib.pyplot as plt
import numpy as np

# Generate some sample data
```

```python
x = np.linspace(0, 10, 100)
y = np.sin(x)

# Create a figure and axis object
fig, ax = plt.subplots()

# Plot the data
ax.plot(x, y)

# Add some labels and a title
ax.set_xlabel('X Label')
ax.set_ylabel('Y Label')
ax.set_title('Sinusoidal Plot')

# Show the plot
plt.show()
```

In this example, we first import the necessary modules (Matplotlib and NumPy). Then, we generate some sample data (an array of 100 x-values evenly spaced between 0 and 10, and an array of the corresponding sine values).

Next, we create a figure and axis object using the **subplots** function. We then use the **plot** function to plot the data on the axis object.

Finally, we add some labels and a title to the plot using the **set_xlabel**, **set_ylabel**, and **set_title** functions. We then use the **show** function to display the plot.

This is just a simple example, and Matplotlib has many more advanced features for creating more complex visualizations.

Pros and Cons

Pros:

- Matplotlib is a widely used and well-established data visualization library for Python, with a large and active community of developers.

- It is highly customizable, allowing users to modify almost every aspect of their plots, including the axes, labels, colors, and styles.

- It provides a wide range of plotting functionality, including line plots, scatter plots, bar charts, histograms, 3D plots, and more.

- Can produce high-quality plots suitable for publication and presentation.

- It is well integrated with other Python libraries for data analysis and scientific computing, such as NumPy, SciPy, and Pandas.

- It is easy to use and learn for basic plotting tasks, making it accessible to users of all levels.

Cons:

- The syntax can be verbose and complex, especially for more advanced customization and plotting tasks.

- The default settings for plots may not always be aesthetically pleasing, and may require additional customization.

- Does not provide as much interactivity or animation functionality as some other data visualization libraries, such as Plotly or Bokeh.

- It can be slower for generating complex or large-scale visualizations compared to some other libraries, such as Seaborn.

- Creating complex or advanced plots may require more coding and effort than with other libraries that provide more specialized plotting functions.

➤ MATPLOTLIB

MACHINE LEARNING

Machine learning is a subfield of artificial intelligence that develops algorithms that can automatically learn and improve from data.

In machine learning, a model is trained on a large dataset of input-output pairs, called a training set, and then used to make predictions on new, unseen data. The goal is to develop a model that can generalize well to new data by learning patterns and relationships in the training data that can be applied to new data.

There are several machine learning types, including **supervised**, **unsupervised**, and **reinforcement learning**. In supervised learning, the training set includes labeled examples of input-output pairs, and the goal is to learn a function that can accurately predict the output for new inputs. In unsupervised learning, the training set does not include labels; the goal is to discover patterns and relationships in the input data. Finally, in reinforcement learning, an agent learns to interact with an environment to achieve a goal by receiving rewards or penalties based on actions.

Machine learning has many applications, from image recognition and natural language processing to recommendation systems and predictive analytics. It is used in various industries, including healthcare, finance, and e-commerce, to automate decision-making, improve efficiency, and gain insights from data.

SCIKIT-LEARN

Python scikit-learn (also known as sklearn) is a popular machine learning library for the Python programming language. It provides a range of supervised and unsupervised learning algorithms for various types of data analysis tasks such as classification, regression, clustering, and dimensionality reduction.

It was developed by David Cournapeau as a Google Summer of Code project in 2007 and is now maintained by a team of developers. It is open-source software and is available under a permissive BSD-style license.

Scikit-learn is built on top of other popular scientific computing libraries for Python, such as NumPy, SciPy, and matplotlib. It also integrates with other machine learning and data analysis libraries such as TensorFlow and Pandas.

Scikit-learn provides a wide range of machine learning algorithms, including:

- **Linear and logistic regression**

- **Support Vector Machines (SVM)**

- **Decision Trees and Random Forests**

- **K-Nearest Neighbors (KNN)**

- **Naive Bayes**

- **Clustering algorithms (e.g. K-Means)**

28

- **Dimensionality reduction techniques (e.g. Principal Component Analysis)**

It also provides utilities for model selection and evaluation, such as cross-validation, grid search, and performance metrics.

Scikit-learn is widely used in academia and industry for a variety of machine learning tasks, such as natural language processing, image recognition, and predictive analytics. It is considered one of the essential tools in the Python data science ecosystem.

An example code snippet that demonstrates how to use scikit-learn to train a simple logistic regression model:

```
from sklearn.linear_model import
LogisticRegression
from sklearn.datasets import load_iris

# Load the iris dataset
iris = load_iris()

# Split the dataset into features (X) and
labels (y)
X, y = iris.data, iris.target

# Create a LogisticRegression object
logreg = LogisticRegression()

# Fit the model using the iris dataset
logreg.fit(X, y)

# Predict the class labels for a new set of
features
new_X = [[5.1, 3.5, 1.4, 0.2], [6.2, 3.4, 5.4,
2.3]]
predicted_y = logreg.predict(new_X)
```

```
print(predicted_y)
```

In this example, we first import the necessary modules from scikit-learn (**LogisticRegression** for the model and **load_iris** for the iris dataset). We then load the iris dataset, which is a well-known dataset in machine learning consisting of 150 samples of iris flowers, with four features each.

We then split the dataset into features (the **X** variable) and labels (the **y** variable). We create a **LogisticRegression** object and fit the model to the dataset using the **fit** function.

Finally, we use the trained model to predict the class labels for two new sets of features (**new_X**). The predicted class labels are printed to the console.

This is just a simple example, and scikit-learn has many more advanced features and models for a wide range of machine learning tasks.

Pros and Cons

Pros:

- It's a powerful and comprehensive machine learning library that offers a wide range of algorithms for various tasks.

- Scikit-learn is easy to use and has a relatively simple API compared to other machine learning libraries.

- It is built on top of other popular scientific computing libraries for Python such as NumPy, SciPy, and matplotlib, which makes it easy to integrate into existing Python data analysis workflows.

- It provides a range of tools for data preprocessing, feature selection, and model evaluation, which can help streamline the machine learning workflow.

- Scikit-learn is well-documented, with comprehensive user guides, API references, and a large online community of users.

- It is open-source and free to use, making it accessible to a wide range of users.

Cons:

- While scikit-learn offers a wide range of algorithms, it may not be the best choice for some specific tasks or datasets that require more specialized algorithms or models.

- It may not be the most efficient library for large-scale or complex machine learning tasks, as it is primarily designed for small to medium-sized datasets.

31

- The simplicity of the scikit-learn API may limit the level of customization and control that more advanced users require.

- It does not include some newer or more advanced machine learning techniques that have been developed more recently, such as deep learning.

- Scikit-learn does not include built-in support for some popular machine learning frameworks such as TensorFlow or PyTorch, which may limit its flexibility in some use cases.

PYTORCH

PyTorch is a popular open-source machine learning library for the Python programming language. It is primarily used for developing deep learning models and provides a range of tools and features for building, training, and deploying neural networks.

It was developed by Facebook's AI research group in 2016 and has quickly become one of the most popular deep learning libraries in the Python ecosystem. It is known for its flexibility and ease-of-use, allowing users to build and train complex neural networks with relatively few lines of code.

PyTorch supports a range of neural network architectures, including convolutional neural networks (CNNs), recurrent neural networks (RNNs), and transformers, and provides a variety of optimization algorithms for training these models, including stochastic gradient descent (SGD) and Adam.

Some of the key features of PyTorch include:

- Automatic differentiation, which allows users to easily compute gradients for neural network models.

- Dynamic computational graphs, which enable more flexibility in building and modifying neural networks.

- A comprehensive tensor library, which provides a range of operations for manipulating multi-dimensional arrays.

- Integration with popular Python libraries such as NumPy and pandas.

- A large and active community of users and developers.

PyTorch is used in a wide range of applications, including computer vision, natural language processing, and reinforcement learning. It is particularly popular among researchers and developers who value its flexibility and ease-of-use.

An example code snippet that demonstrates how to use PyTorch to define and train a simple neural network to classify handwritten digits:

```python
import torch
import torch.nn as nn
import torch.optim as optim
from torchvision import datasets, transforms

# Define a neural network
class Net(nn.Module):
    def __init__(self):
        super(Net, self).__init__()
        self.fc1 = nn.Linear(784, 64)
        self.fc2 = nn.Linear(64, 10)
        self.relu = nn.ReLU()

    def forward(self, x):
        x = self.relu(self.fc1(x))
        x = self.fc2(x)
        return x
```

```python
# Load the MNIST dataset
transform =
transforms.Compose([transforms.ToTensor(),

transforms.Normalize((0.1307,), (0.3081,))])
trainset = datasets.MNIST(root='./data',
train=True, download=True, transform=transform)
testset = datasets.MNIST(root='./data',
train=False, download=True,
transform=transform)
trainloader =
torch.utils.data.DataLoader(trainset,
batch_size=32, shuffle=True)
testloader =
torch.utils.data.DataLoader(testset,
batch_size=32, shuffle=False)

# Create a neural network object and an
optimizer
net = Net()
optimizer = optim.SGD(net.parameters(),
lr=0.01, momentum=0.9)

# Train the neural network
criterion = nn.CrossEntropyLoss()
for epoch in range(10):
    running_loss = 0.0
    for i, data in enumerate(trainloader, 0):
        inputs, labels = data
        inputs = inputs.view(-1, 28*28)
        optimizer.zero_grad()
        outputs = net(inputs)
        loss = criterion(outputs, labels)
        loss.backward()
        optimizer.step()
        running_loss += loss.item()
    print(f"Epoch {epoch+1}, Loss:
{running_loss / len(trainloader)}")

# Test the neural network
```

```
correct = 0
total = 0
with torch.no_grad():
    for data in testloader:
        inputs, labels = data
        inputs = inputs.view(-1, 28*28)
        outputs = net(inputs)
        _, predicted = torch.max(outputs.data,
1)
        total += labels.size(0)
        correct += (predicted ==
labels).sum().item()
print(f"Accuracy: {correct / total}")
```

In this example, we first import the necessary modules from PyTorch, including **torch, torch.nn, torch.optim**, and **torchvision**. We then define a simple neural network architecture using the **nn.Module** class, which includes two fully connected layers and a ReLU activation function.

We then load the MNIST dataset using the **torchvision.datasets** module and create data loaders to iterate over the data during training and testing. We create a neural network object and an optimizer using the **optim** module, and define the loss function using the **nn.CrossEntropyLoss** class.

We then train the neural network for 10 epochs using a batch size of 32, computing the loss using the specified criterion and backpropagating the gradients using the optimizer.

Finally, we test the trained neural network using the test data, computing the accuracy of the model on the test set.

This is just a simple example, and PyTorch has many more advanced features and models for a wide range of deep learning tasks.

Pros and Cons

Pros:

- It is known for its ease-of-use and flexibility, allowing users to quickly build and train complex neural networks with relatively few lines of code.

- It includes a range of tools and features for deep learning, including automatic differentiation, dynamic computational graphs, and a comprehensive tensor library.

- Integrates well with other popular Python libraries such as NumPy and pandas, making it easy to use in conjunction with other data analysis and machine learning tools.

- It has a large and active community of users and developers, which means that there is a lot of support and resources available for users who are new to the library or who need help with more advanced tasks.

- PyTorch is used widely in both academia and industry, and has been used to achieve state-of-the-art results in a variety of deep learning tasks.

Cons:

- It may not be as fast or efficient as other deep learning libraries such as TensorFlow or Keras, particularly for large-scale distributed training.

- Can be less stable than other deep learning libraries, which can make it more difficult to debug errors or reproduce results.

- May require more expertise and experience to use effectively than other deep learning libraries, particularly for users who are new to machine learning or who are not familiar with Python programming.

TENSORFLOW

TensorFlow is a popular open-source machine learning library developed by Google. It is primarily used for building and training deep neural networks, although it also includes a range of tools and features for other machine learning tasks.

It was originally developed by the Google Brain team for internal use, but was later released as an open-source library in 2015. Since then, it has become one of the most widely used and respected machine learning libraries, with a large and active community of users and developers.

TensorFlow is designed to be flexible and scalable, allowing users to build and train deep neural networks on a wide range of hardware, from laptops and mobile devices to large-scale distributed clusters. It includes a comprehensive tensor library for efficient numerical computations, as well as a range of high-level APIs for building and training neural networks.

It also includes a range of tools and features for data preprocessing, visualization, and analysis, making it a comprehensive and powerful machine learning platform. It has been used widely in both academia and industry to achieve state-of-the-art results in a variety of machine learning tasks, including image recognition, natural language processing, and more.

Overall, TensorFlow is a powerful and flexible machine learning library that is widely used and respected in the machine learning community.

39

An example code snippet that uses TensorFlow to train a simple neural network for classifying handwritten digits from the MNIST dataset:

```python
import tensorflow as tf
from tensorflow.keras.datasets import mnist

# Load the MNIST dataset
(x_train, y_train), (x_test, y_test) =
mnist.load_data()

# Preprocess the data
x_train = x_train / 255.0
x_test = x_test / 255.0

# Define the model architecture
model = tf.keras.models.Sequential([
    tf.keras.layers.Flatten(input_shape=(28,
28)),
    tf.keras.layers.Dense(128,
activation='relu'),
    tf.keras.layers.Dense(10)
])

# Compile the model
model.compile(optimizer='adam',

loss=tf.keras.losses.SparseCategoricalCrossentr
opy(from_logits=True),
                metrics=['accuracy'])

# Train the model
model.fit(x_train, y_train, epochs=10,
validation_data=(x_test, y_test))

# Evaluate the model
test_loss, test_acc = model.evaluate(x_test,
y_test, verbose=2)
print('Test accuracy:', test_acc)
```

This code first loads the MNIST dataset and preprocesses the data by scaling it to the range [0, 1]. It then defines a simple neural network architecture using the Keras API within TensorFlow, with a single hidden layer containing 128 neurons and ReLU activation, and an output layer containing 10 neurons (one for each possible digit). The model is then compiled with the Adam optimizer and Sparse Categorical Crossentropy loss, and is trained for 10 epochs on the training data, with validation performed on the test data after each epoch. Finally, the model is evaluated on the test data and the test accuracy is printed.

Note that this is just a simple example - TensorFlow is capable of much more complex models and architectures for a wide range of machine learning tasks.

Pros and Cons

Pros:

- Is widely considered to be one of the most powerful and flexible machine learning libraries available, with a range of tools and features for building and training complex neural networks.

- It has a large and active community of users and developers, which means that there is a lot of support and resources available for users who are new to the library or who need help with more advanced tasks.

- It is designed to be scalable and efficient, allowing users to build and train models on a wide range of hardware, from laptops to large-scale distributed clusters.

- Includes a comprehensive tensor library for efficient numerical computations, as well as a range of high-level APIs for building and training neural networks.

- Has been used widely in both academia and industry to achieve state-of-the-art results in a variety of machine learning tasks, including image recognition, natural language processing, and more.

Cons:

- Can have a steeper learning curve than other machine learning libraries, particularly for users who are new to deep learning or who are not familiar with Python programming.

- It can be less intuitive than other machine learning libraries, with a more verbose and complex syntax.

- TensorFlow's low-level API can require more code to accomplish simple tasks than other machine learning libraries, which can make it less attractive for prototyping or experimentation.

- It's computational graph architecture can make debugging more difficult, particularly for users who are not familiar with the internals of the library.

- TensorFlow's computational graph architecture can make it harder to integrate with other Python libraries, although this has been improving with recent releases.

XGBOOST

XGBoost is an open-source software library which provides a gradient boosting framework for machine learning. It was developed by Tianqi Chen and his colleagues at the University of Washington and is now maintained by DMLC. XGBoost is designed to be scalable, portable and efficient, making it popular for use in a wide range of applications, including prediction, classification, and ranking problems in industry and academia.

In Python, XGBoost can be used via the **xgboost** library, which provides an API for defining, training, and evaluating XGBoost models. The library is built on top of the core C++ XGBoost library, which provides a fast and efficient implementation of gradient boosting.

It works by iteratively adding decision trees to a model, with each tree trained to correct the errors of the previous trees. The algorithm combines the predictions of all the trees to produce a final prediction. XGBoost uses a variety of optimization techniques, including regularization and parallel processing, to improve the accuracy and speed of the model.

It has become a popular tool for use in machine learning competitions, due to its ability to achieve state-of-the-art performance on a wide range of tasks.

- The library provides a variety of hyperparameters that can be tuned to improve model performance and adapt to different use cases.

- XGBoost is an open-source library with an active development community, which means that it is constantly being updated and improved.

Cons:

- Is primarily designed for structured data and may not be as effective for unstructured data such as text or image data.

- The hyperparameter tuning process can be time-consuming and requires some level of expertise to optimize the model effectively.

- May not be suitable for real-time or online learning applications, as it requires retraining the entire model every time new data is added.

- Since XGBoost is a gradient boosting algorithm, it is susceptible to the same issues as other gradient boosting algorithms, such as being prone to overfitting and requiring careful regularization to prevent this.

LIGHTGBM

Python LightGBM is a gradient boosting framework that uses tree-based learning algorithms. It is a powerful machine learning library that was developed by Microsoft and is designed to be efficient and fast. LightGBM stands for "Light Gradient Boosting Machine". It was developed to tackle large-scale data and can handle millions of rows and thousands of features.

LightGBM differs from other gradient boosting libraries, such as XGBoost, by using a novel technique called "Gradient-based One-Side Sampling" (GOSS) and "Exclusive Feature Bundling" (EFB). These techniques help to reduce the computational resources required for training the model and to speed up the training process.

It supports various types of learning tasks, such as regression, classification, and ranking. It also has many useful features, such as built-in cross-validation, early stopping, and support for categorical features.

Overall, LightGBM is a powerful library for gradient boosting and is an excellent choice for handling large-scale structured data.

An example code usage of LightGBM in Python for a binary classification problem:

```python
import lightgbm as lgb
from sklearn.datasets import load_breast_cancer
from sklearn.model_selection import train_test_split
from sklearn.metrics import accuracy_score
```

```python
# Load the breast cancer dataset
data = load_breast_cancer()

# Split the data into training and testing sets
X_train, X_test, y_train, y_test =
train_test_split(data.data, data.target,
test_size=0.2, random_state=42)

# Convert the data into LightGBM's dataset
format
train_data = lgb.Dataset(X_train,
label=y_train)
test_data = lgb.Dataset(X_test, label=y_test)

# Set the hyperparameters for the LightGBM
model
params = {
    'objective': 'binary',
    'metric': 'binary_logloss',
    'num_leaves': 31,
    'learning_rate': 0.05,
    'feature_fraction': 0.9
}

# Train the LightGBM model on the training data
num_rounds = 100
model = lgb.train(params, train_data,
num_rounds)

# Make predictions on the testing data
y_pred = model.predict(X_test)
y_pred = [1 if x >= 0.5 else 0 for x in y_pred]

# Evaluate the accuracy of the model
accuracy = accuracy_score(y_test, y_pred)
print("Accuracy: {:.2f}%".format(accuracy *
100))
```

In this example, we start by loading the breast cancer dataset using scikit-learn's **load_breast_cancer** function.

We then split the dataset into training and testing sets using scikit-learn's **train_test_split** function.

Next, we convert the training and testing data into LightGBM's dataset format using the **lgb.Dataset** class. We then set the hyperparameters for the LightGBM model, including the objective function, the evaluation metric, the number of leaves in each tree, the learning rate, and the feature fraction.

We then train the LightGBM model on the training data using the **lgb.train** function. Once the model is trained, we use it to make predictions on the testing data by calling the **predict** method. We then convert the predicted probabilities into binary predictions by setting a threshold of 0.5.

Finally, we evaluate the accuracy of the model by comparing the predicted labels to the true labels in the testing set, and print out the accuracy score.

Pros and Cons

Pros:

- LightGBM is designed to handle large-scale data and can handle millions of rows and thousands of features efficiently.

- It uses a novel technique called "Gradient-based One-Side Sampling" (GOSS) and "Exclusive Feature Bundling" (EFB) to reduce the computational resources required for training the model and to speed up the training process.

- It supports various types of learning tasks, such as regression, classification, and ranking.

- It has many useful features, such as built-in cross-validation, early stopping, and support for categorical features.

- It has a good accuracy and performance compared to other gradient boosting frameworks.

Cons:

- LightGBM may require some hyperparameter tuning to achieve optimal results.

- It may be more difficult to use and understand compared to simpler machine learning algorithms, especially for beginners.

- The library does not support GPU acceleration by default, which may be a disadvantage for some use cases where GPU acceleration is desired. However, there are ways to use LightGBM with GPU acceleration through third-party libraries.

KERAS

Keras is a high-level neural networks API, written in Python and capable of running on top of popular deep learning frameworks such as TensorFlow. Keras was designed to enable fast experimentation with deep neural networks, and it has become one of the most popular deep learning libraries. It is particularly well-suited for building and training deep learning models for computer vision and natural language processing (NLP) tasks. Keras is open-source and is maintained by a community of contributors on GitHub.

An example code for building a simple neural network using Keras:

```python
import numpy as np
from keras.models import Sequential
from keras.layers import Dense

# Generate some dummy data for training and
testing
x_train = np.random.random((1000, 10))
y_train = np.random.randint(2, size=(1000, 1))
x_test = np.random.random((100, 10))
y_test = np.random.randint(2, size=(100, 1))

# Build the model
model = Sequential()
model.add(Dense(32, input_dim=10,
activation='relu'))
model.add(Dense(1, activation='sigmoid'))

# Compile the model
model.compile(optimizer='rmsprop',
loss='binary_crossentropy',
metrics=['accuracy'])
```

52

```
# Train the model
model.fit(x_train, y_train, epochs=20,
batch_size=32)

# Evaluate the model on the test data
score = model.evaluate(x_test, y_test,
batch_size=128)

# Print the test loss and accuracy
print('Test loss:', score[0])
print('Test accuracy:', score[1])
```

This code defines a simple neural network with one hidden layer of 32 neurons and an output layer with one neuron, which is used for binary classification. The model is compiled with the binary crossentropy loss function and the RMSprop optimizer. It is then trained on some randomly generated training data for 20 epochs, with a batch size of 32. Finally, the model is evaluated on some randomly generated test data, and the test loss and accuracy are printed.

Pros and Cons

Pros:

- User-friendly API: Keras provides a simple and intuitive interface that makes it easy to use and understand, especially for beginners in deep learning.

- Modular and flexible architecture: Keras allows users to build models by stacking multiple layers, which can be easily added or removed, allowing for quick experimentation and prototyping.

- Wide range of applications: Keras supports a variety of deep learning tasks such as image classification, natural language processing, and time series forecasting.

- Efficient computation: Keras can run on both CPUs and GPUs, providing fast computation for large datasets.

Cons:

- Limited flexibility: While Keras is great for prototyping and experimenting, it may not provide the level of flexibility and control needed for more complex deep learning models.

- Less customization: Keras abstracts many of the lower-level implementation details, which can limit customization options for advanced users.

- Limited backward compatibility: Keras has undergone some significant changes over time, which can make it challenging to maintain backward compatibility between different versions.

- Limited support for distributed training: While Keras can be used for distributed training, it may not be as efficient as other deep learning frameworks specifically designed for distributed computing.

PYCARET

PyCaret is an open-source machine learning library in Python that automates the end-to-end machine learning process. It is designed to be an easy-to-use library that requires minimal coding effort while providing maximum flexibility and control to the user. PyCaret has a wide range of features, including data preprocessing, classification, regression, clustering, anomaly detection, natural language processing, time series forecasting, and model deployment.

It is built on top of popular machine learning libraries such as scikit-learn, XGBoost, LightGBM, CatBoost, and spaCy. It provides a high-level API that simplifies complex machine learning workflows by automating repetitive tasks, such as data preprocessing, hyperparameter tuning, model selection, and ensemble building.

PyCaret is particularly useful for data scientists and machine learning practitioners who want to quickly build and prototype machine learning models without having to spend a lot of time on data preprocessing and model selection. It is also suitable for business analysts and data engineers who want to explore and analyze data using machine learning techniques.

An example code usage of PyCaret:

```python
from pycaret.datasets import get_data
from pycaret.classification import *

# load data
data = get_data('diabetes')
```

```
# setup model
clf = setup(data, target='Class variable')

# compare models
compare_models()
```

In this example, we first import the **get_data** function from **pycaret.datasets** and the **setup** function, as well as the **compare_models** function, from **pycaret.classification**. We then load the 'diabetes' dataset using **get_data**, and set up the classification model using **setup**, specifying the target variable to be 'Class variable'. Finally, we compare the performance of different classification models using **compare_models**.

Note that **setup** automatically preprocesses the data, performs feature engineering and selection, and sets up the training and testing environment. **compare_models** returns a table of the cross-validated performance metrics for each model, which can be used to select the best-performing model for further tuning and evaluation.

Pros and Cons

Pros:

- Provides a wide range of built-in functions for data preparation, model training, hyperparameter tuning, and model deployment, which makes it easy to quickly build and test machine learning models.

- Supports a wide range of machine learning models and algorithms, including both supervised and unsupervised learning methods.

- Provides extensive documentation and examples, making it easy to learn and use for both beginners and experienced machine learning practitioners.

- PyCaret provides a web-based interface for building and deploying machine learning models, which can be particularly useful for non-technical users who want to use machine learning without having to write any code.

Cons:

- PyCaret's ease of use and built-in functionality may come at the cost of flexibility and customizability, particularly for advanced machine learning tasks that require more complex data processing or modeling techniques.

- May not be the best choice for large-scale or high-performance machine learning tasks that require specialized hardware or software.

- Is a relatively new library, so it may not have the same level of community support or third-party integrations as more established machine learning libraries.

➤ PYCARET

MLOPS

MLOps (Machine Learning Operations) is a set of practices and tools that streamline the machine learning (ML) development lifecycle, from development to deployment and maintenance.

It is similar to DevOps, a set of practices for developing, deploying, and maintaining software applications. However, MLOps is tailored to the specific needs and challenges of developing and deploying machine learning models.

It involves various tasks, including data preparation and cleaning, model training and validation, model deployment and serving, and monitoring and maintenance. It also requires collaboration between different teams, such as data scientists, machine learning engineers, software developers, and operations teams.

MLOps tools and practices include version control systems, continuous integration, and deployment (CI/CD) pipelines, containerization, orchestration tools, and monitoring and logging tools. By implementing MLOps, organizations can improve their machine-learning systems' speed, scalability, and reliability and reduce the risk of errors or failures in production.

MLFLOW

MLflow is an open-source platform for managing and tracking machine learning experiments. It provides a simple and flexible interface for tracking experiments, packaging code into reproducible runs, and sharing and deploying models.

MLflow was developed by Databricks and released as an open-source project in 2018. The goal of MLflow is to simplify the machine learning lifecycle by providing a standardized way to manage and track experiments, as well as to package and deploy models. MLflow can be used with a variety of machine learning libraries and frameworks, including TensorFlow, PyTorch, and scikit-learn.

MLflow consists of several components:

1. Tracking: a module for logging and tracking experiments, including parameters, metrics, and artifacts.

2. Projects: a format for packaging data science code in a reusable and reproducible way.

3. Models: a format for packaging machine learning models in a way that can be easily deployed to a variety of production environments.

4. Model Registry: a centralized repository for managing models, including versioning, stage transitions, and access control.

MLflow also provides a command-line interface and APIs for integrating with other tools and workflows. Overall, MLflow aims to simplify the process of developing, training, and deploying machine learning models, while improving collaboration and reproducibility

An example code snippet that uses MLflow to track and log metrics during a machine learning experiment:

```python
import mlflow
import numpy as np
from sklearn.linear_model import
LinearRegression

# Start an MLflow experiment
mlflow.set_experiment("linear-regression")

# Generate some random data
x = np.random.rand(100, 1)
y = 2*x + np.random.randn(100, 1)

# Define a model
model = LinearRegression()

# Train the model
model.fit(x, y)

# Log some metrics
mlflow.log_metric("r2_score", model.score(x,
y))
mlflow.log_metric("mse",
np.mean((model.predict(x) - y) ** 2))

# Save the model
mlflow.sklearn.log_model(model, "model")

# End the experiment
mlflow.end_experiment()
```

61

In this example, we first start an MLflow experiment by calling **mlflow.set_experiment** with a name for the experiment. We then generate some random data and define a linear regression model using scikit-learn. We train the model on the data, and then use MLflow to log some metrics (the R-squared score and mean squared error) using **mlflow.log_metric**. We also save the trained model using **mlflow.sklearn.log_model**. Finally, we end the experiment using **mlflow.end_experiment**.

By running this code, we can use the MLflow UI to view and compare the results of multiple experiments, including the logged metrics and the trained models.

Pros and Cons

Pros:

1. Reproducibility: MLflow provides a standardized way to track experiments, packages, and deploy models, which can help ensure that experiments are reproducible.

2. Flexibility: MLflow can be used with a variety of machine learning libraries and frameworks, including TensorFlow, PyTorch, and scikit-learn, making it a versatile tool for managing machine learning projects.

3. Collaboration: MLflow provides a centralized platform for sharing experiments, models, and code, which can improve collaboration among data scientists and developers.

4. Visualization: MLflow provides a web-based UI for visualizing and comparing experiments, which can help with debugging and optimization.

Cons:

1. Learning Curve: MLflow requires some learning to use effectively, including knowledge of the MLflow API and how to integrate it with your existing workflows.

2. Overhead: Using MLflow requires some additional overhead compared to simply running experiments and tracking results manually, although this overhead is typically minimal.

3. Limitations: While MLflow is a powerful tool, it may not meet all the needs of a particular project, such as specialized requirements for model deployment or training.

MLflow can be a valuable tool for managing and tracking machine learning projects, especially in environments where collaboration and reproducibility are important. However, like any tool, it has its strengths and weaknesses, and should be evaluated based on the specific needs of a project.

KUBEFLOW

Kubeflow is an open-source platform for running machine learning workloads on Kubernetes. Kubernetes is a container orchestration platform that provides a scalable and resilient infrastructure for deploying and managing distributed applications. Kubeflow builds on top of Kubernetes to provide a platform for deploying, scaling, and managing machine learning workloads.

Kubeflow provides a range of tools and frameworks for building and deploying machine learning models, including:

1. Jupyter notebooks: A web-based environment for interactive data analysis and model development.

2. TensorFlow: A popular machine learning library for building and training deep neural networks.

3. PyTorch: A popular machine learning library for building and training deep neural networks.

4. Apache Spark: A distributed computing framework for processing large datasets.

5. Apache Beam: A unified programming model for processing both batch and streaming data.

Kubeflow also provides a range of components for managing the machine learning workflow, including:

1. Pipelines: A tool for building, deploying, and managing machine learning pipelines.

2. Training: A tool for managing distributed training jobs on Kubernetes.

3. Serving: A tool for deploying and serving trained models as web services.

4. Metadata: A tool for tracking and managing the metadata associated with machine learning experiments.

Kubeflow provides a powerful platform for building and deploying machine learning workloads on Kubernetes. By leveraging the scalability and resilience of Kubernetes, Kubeflow can help streamline the machine learning workflow and improve the reproducibility and scalability of machine learning models.

An example code snippet that demonstrates how to use Kubeflow to train a TensorFlow model on a Kubernetes cluster:

```python
import kfp
import kfp.dsl as dsl
import kfp.components as comp

# Define the pipeline
@dsl.pipeline(name='train-tf-model',
description='Trains a TensorFlow model on
Kubernetes')
def train_pipeline(
    data_path: str,
    model_path: str,
    epochs: int,
    batch_size: int,
    learning_rate: float
):
    # Load the data
    load_data = dsl.ContainerOp(
        name='load_data',
        image='my-registry/my-image',
```

```
        command=['python',
'/app/load_data.py'],
        arguments=[
            '--data-path', data_path,
            '--output-path',
'/mnt/data/raw_data.csv'
        ]
    )

    # Preprocess the data
    preprocess = dsl.ContainerOp(
        name='preprocess',
        image='my-registry/my-image',
        command=['python',
'/app/preprocess.py'],
        arguments=[
            '--data-path',
'/mnt/data/raw_data.csv',
            '--output-path',
'/mnt/data/cleaned_data.csv'
        ]
    ).after(load_data)

    # Train the model
    train = dsl.ContainerOp(
        name='train',
        image='my-registry/my-image',
        command=['python', '/app/train.py'],
        arguments=[
            '--train-data',
'/mnt/data/cleaned_data.csv',
            '--model-dir', model_path,
            '--epochs', epochs,
            '--batch-size', batch_size,
            '--learning-rate', learning_rate
        ]
    ).after(preprocess)

# Compile the pipeline
pipeline_func = train_pipeline
```

```python
pipeline_filename = pipeline_func.__name__ +
'.yaml'
kfp.compiler.Compiler().compile(pipeline_func,
pipeline_filename)

# Define the Kubeflow experiment
experiment_name = 'train-tf-model'
run_name = pipeline_func.__name__ + ' run'
client = kfp.Client()

# Define the pipeline parameters
params = {
    'data_path': 'gs://my-bucket/my-data.csv',
    'model_path': 'gs://my-bucket/my-model',
    'epochs': 10,
    'batch_size': 32,
    'learning_rate': 0.001
}

# Submit the pipeline to the Kubeflow cluster
try:
    experiment =
client.create_experiment(name=experiment_name)
except kfp.errors.ApiException:
    experiment =
client.get_experiment(experiment_name)
run = client.run_pipeline(experiment.id,
run_name, pipeline_filename, params)
```

In this example, we define a Kubeflow pipeline that consists of two components: a component for preprocessing the data and a component for training the model. We then define the pipeline itself, which takes as input the path to the raw data, the path where the trained model will be saved, and various hyperparameters for the training process. The pipeline first preprocesses the data using the **preprocess_op** component, then trains the model using the **train_op** component. Finally, we compile the pipeline and submit it to the Kubeflow cluster using the **kfp.Client** class.

By running this code, we can train a TensorFlow model on a Kubernetes cluster using Kubeflow, while also benefiting from the scalability, fault-tolerance, and reproducibility provided by Kubernetes.

Pros and Cons

Pros:

1. Scalability: Kubeflow is designed to work with Kubernetes, which provides a scalable and distributed environment for running machine learning workloads. This means that Kubeflow can easily scale to handle large datasets and complex models.

2. Reproducibility: Kubeflow enables you to create reproducible pipelines for your machine learning workflows, which ensures that your experiments are repeatable and your results are reliable. This is because Kubeflow makes it easy to track and version your data, code, and configurations.

3. Portability: Kubeflow allows you to build machine learning pipelines that can be run on any Kubernetes cluster, whether on-premises or in the cloud. This means that you can easily move your machine learning workloads between different environments without having to change your code or configurations.

68

4. Customizability: Kubeflow provides a range of pre-built components for common machine learning tasks, but it also allows you to create your own custom components using any programming language or tool. This makes it easy to tailor your machine learning pipelines to your specific needs.

Cons:

1. Complexity: Kubeflow is a complex system that requires a significant amount of configuration and setup to get started. This can be a barrier to entry for smaller teams or organizations that don't have dedicated DevOps resources.

2. Learning curve: Kubeflow is a relatively new technology, and as such, it has a steep learning curve. This means that it can take some time for teams to become proficient in using Kubeflow for their machine learning workflows.

3. Resource requirements: Because Kubeflow is designed to run on Kubernetes, it requires a significant amount of resources to run effectively. This means that teams will need to have access to a Kubernetes cluster, which can be a challenge for smaller organizations or teams without dedicated DevOps resources.

4. Versioning: While Kubeflow does provide tools for versioning data and code, there can be challenges with versioning models and configurations. This can make it difficult to track changes to models

over time and ensure that models are reproducible.

ZENML

ZENML is an open-source MLOps framework that provides a pipeline-based approach for managing end-to-end machine learning workflows. ZENML is designed to simplify the development and deployment of machine learning models by providing a high-level API for common machine learning tasks.

It is built on top of TensorFlow and is designed to integrate seamlessly with popular machine learning libraries such as scikit-learn and PyTorch. ZENML supports a range of data sources and preprocessing techniques, and provides a range of pre-built components for common machine learning tasks such as data validation, feature engineering, and model training.

It also provides a range of features for managing the deployment and monitoring of machine learning models, including support for model versioning, A/B testing, and automated model retraining.

ZENML is designed to be flexible and customizable, allowing users to create custom components using any programming language or tool. ZENML also provides extensive documentation and a range of tutorials to help users get started with the framework.

An example code usage of ZENML for an MLOps workflow:

```
from zenml.core import SimplePipeline
from zenml.datasources import CSVDatasource
from zenml.steps.evaluator.tf_evaluator import
TFEvaluator
```

71

```python
from zenml.steps.preprocesser.standard_scaler
import StandardScaler
from zenml.steps.splitter.random_split import
RandomSplit
from zenml.steps.trainer.tf_trainer import
TFTrainer
from
zenml.backends.orchestrator.tf_local_orchestrat
or import TFLocalOrchestrator

# Define data source
ds = CSVDatasource(name='my-csv-datasource',
path='./my-dataset.csv')

# Define splitter
split = RandomSplit(split_map={'train': 0.7,
'eval': 0.2, 'test': 0.1})

# Define preprocesser
preprocesser = StandardScaler()

# Define trainer
trainer = TFTrainer(
    loss='categorical_crossentropy',
    last_activation='softmax',
    epochs=10,
    batch_size=32
)

# Define evaluator
evaluator = TFEvaluator()

# Define pipeline
pipeline = SimplePipeline(
    datasource=ds,
    splitter=split,
    preprocesser=preprocesser,
    trainer=trainer,
    evaluator=evaluator,
    name='my-pipeline'
)
```

```
# Define orchestrator
orchestrator = TFLocalOrchestrator()

# Run pipeline
orchestrator.run(pipeline)
```

In this example, we first define a **CSVDatasource** that points to a CSV file containing our dataset. We then define a **RandomSplit** splitter to split the dataset into training, evaluation, and testing sets.

Next, we define a **StandardScaler** preprocesser to standardize the features in the dataset. We then define a **TFTrainer** to train a TensorFlow model on the preprocessed data.

We also define a **TFEvaluator** to evaluate the trained model on the evaluation set.

Finally, we create a **SimplePipeline** object that incorporates all of the defined steps, and we define a **TFLocalOrchestrator** to run the pipeline locally.

We then run the pipeline using the **orchestrator.run(pipeline)** command. This will execute the pipeline steps in the order defined and output the results of the pipeline. This pipeline can then be versioned, deployed, and managed using the ZENML framework.

Pros and Cons

Pros:

- Pipeline-based approach: ZENML provides a pipeline-based approach to managing end-to-end machine learning workflows, making it easy to create, test, and deploy machine learning models.

- Flexibility: ZENML is designed to be flexible and customizable, allowing users to create custom components using any programming language or tool. This makes it easy to integrate ZENML with other tools and libraries that you may already be using.

- Scalability: ZENML is designed to be scalable, and can be run on a range of different compute environments, from a single machine to a distributed cluster.

- Integration with TensorFlow: ZENML is built on top of TensorFlow, one of the most popular deep learning libraries. This makes it easy to incorporate TensorFlow models into your ZENML pipelines, and provides a range of pre-built TensorFlow components that can be used in your pipelines.

- Open-source: ZENML is an open-source framework, meaning that it is freely available for anyone to use, modify, and contribute to.

Cons:

- Learning curve: Like any new tool or library, there may be a learning curve involved in using ZENML, particularly if you are not familiar with the pipeline-based approach to managing machine learning workflows.

- Limited community support: As a relatively new open-source project, ZENML may have limited community support compared to more established MLOps frameworks like Kubeflow.

- Limited pre-built components: While ZENML provides a range of pre-built components for common machine learning tasks like data preprocessing and model training, the selection of components is more limited compared to some other MLOps frameworks.

- Dependency on TensorFlow: While ZENML's integration with TensorFlow is a strength, it can also be a weakness for users who prefer to use other machine learning libraries or tools.

> ZENML

EXPLAINABLE AI

Explainable AI (XAI) is a set of techniques and practices that aim to make machine learning models and their decisions more transparent and understandable to humans.

XAI aims to provide insights into how a machine learning model works, how it makes decisions, and what factors influence its predictions. This is important because many modern machine learning models are complex and challenging to interpret, and their choices may significantly impact individuals and society.

XAI techniques include feature importance analysis, local and global model interpretability, counterfactual analysis, and model visualization. These techniques can help to identify the most critical factors that influence a model's predictions, provide explanations for specific predictions, and highlight potential biases or inaccuracies in the model.

Explainable AI is particularly important in applications where decisions made by machine learning models have significant consequences, such as healthcare, finance, and criminal justice. By making machine learning models more transparent and understandable, XAI can help build trust and confidence in these systems and ensure that they make fair and ethical decisions.

SHAP

SHAP (SHapley Additive exPlanations) is a popular open-source library for interpreting and explaining the predictions of machine learning models. SHAP is based on the concept of Shapley values, which are a method from cooperative game theory used to determine the contribution of each player to a cooperative game. In the context of machine learning, SHAP computes the contribution of each feature to a particular prediction, providing insight into how the model is making its predictions.

It provides a range of tools for visualizing and interpreting model predictions, including summary plots, force plots, and dependence plots. It can be used with a wide range of machine learning models, including both black box and white box models.

Overall, Python SHAP is a powerful tool for understanding how machine learning models are making their predictions, and can be useful in a range of applications, including feature selection, model debugging, and model governance.

An example code usage of Python SHAP:

```python
import shap
from sklearn.ensemble import RandomForestClassifier
from sklearn.datasets import load_breast_cancer

# Load the Breast Cancer Wisconsin dataset
data = load_breast_cancer()
```

```
# Create a random forest classifier
clf = RandomForestClassifier(n_estimators=100,
random_state=0)

# Train the classifier on the breast cancer
dataset
clf.fit(data.data, data.target)

# Initialize the SHAP explainer
explainer = shap.Explainer(clf)

# Generate SHAP values for the first 5
instances in the dataset
shap_values = explainer(data.data[:5])

# Plot the SHAP values for the first instance
shap.plots.waterfall(shap_values[0])
```

In this example, we first load the Breast Cancer Wisconsin dataset and create a random forest classifier using the **RandomForestClassifier** class from scikit-learn. We then train the classifier on the dataset.

Next, we initialize a SHAP explainer using the **Explainer** class from the **shap** library. We then generate SHAP values for the first 5 instances in the dataset using the explainer.

Finally, we plot the SHAP values for the first instance using the **waterfall** function from the **shap.plots** module. This generates a waterfall plot showing the contribution of each feature to the model's prediction for the first instance.

This is just a simple example of how SHAP can be used to interpret the predictions of a machine learning model. In practice, SHAP can be used with a wide range of machine learning models and datasets, and can provide valuable insights into how these models are making their predictions.

Pros and Cons

Pros:

- Provides a powerful tool for interpreting and explaining the predictions of machine learning models.

- Works with a wide range of machine learning models, including black box models.

- Can be used for a variety of tasks, including feature selection, model debugging, and model governance.

- Provides a range of visualizations for exploring and interpreting model predictions.

- Based on a well-established concept from cooperative game theory (Shapley values).

- Has an active community and is widely used in industry and academia.

Cons:

- Can be computationally intensive, especially for large datasets or complex models.

- Can be difficult to interpret and understand, especially for users who are not familiar with the underlying concepts and methods.

- Requires some knowledge of Python and machine learning concepts to use effectively.

- Can be sensitive to the choice of hyperparameters and other settings.

- May not always provide clear or definitive explanations for model predictions.

SHAP is a powerful and widely-used tool for interpreting and explaining machine learning models. However, as with any tool, it has its limitations and requires some expertise to use effectively. It is important to carefully consider the trade-offs and limitations of any model interpretability tool when choosing the right one for a particular application.

LIME

Python LIME (Local Interpretable Model-Agnostic Explanations) is an open-source library for explaining the predictions of machine learning models. Like Python SHAP, LIME provides a way to understand how a model is making its predictions by generating explanations for individual instances. However, while SHAP provides global feature importance measures, LIME generates local explanations that are specific to a particular instance.

It works by training an interpretable model (e.g. a linear model or decision tree) on a sample of instances that are similar to the instance being explained. The interpretable model is then used to generate explanations for the predictions of the original model. This process is repeated for each instance being explained, resulting in local, instance-specific explanations.

LIME can be used with a variety of machine learning models and can provide useful insights into how these models are making their predictions. It can be especially useful when working with black box models or when global feature importance measures are not sufficient for understanding individual predictions.

Overall, Python LIME is a powerful tool for interpreting and explaining machine learning models, especially in cases where SHAP and other global interpretability methods may not be sufficient. It can be used in a variety of applications, including model debugging, model governance, and feature selection.

An example code usage of Python LIME:

```python
from lime import lime_text
from sklearn.pipeline import make_pipeline
from sklearn.ensemble import
RandomForestClassifier
from sklearn.feature_extraction.text import
TfidfVectorizer

# Define a dataset of text documents and
corresponding labels
docs = ['The quick brown fox', 'Jumped over the
lazy dog', 'The dog chased the cat', 'The cat
ran away']
labels = [1, 0, 1, 0]

# Define a random forest classifier and a TF-
IDF vectorizer
clf = RandomForestClassifier(n_estimators=100,
random_state=0)
vectorizer = TfidfVectorizer()

# Train the classifier on the text data
X_train = vectorizer.fit_transform(docs)
clf.fit(X_train, labels)

# Define a LIME explainer for text data
explainer =
lime_text.LimeTextExplainer(class_names=['negat
ive', 'positive'])

# Generate an explanation for the first
document
exp = explainer.explain_instance(docs[0],
clf.predict_proba, num_features=6)

# Print the explanation
print(exp.as_list())
```

In this example, we define a dataset of text documents and corresponding labels. We then define a random forest classifier and a TF-IDF vectorizer, and train the classifier on the text data.

Next, we define a LIME explainer for text data using the **LimeTextExplainer** class from the **lime** library. We then generate an explanation for the first document using the explainer.

Finally, we print the explanation using the **as_list** method of the explanation object. This generates a list of features and their corresponding weights, indicating the contribution of each feature to the model's prediction for the first document.

This is just a simple example of how LIME can be used to interpret the predictions of a machine learning model on text data. In practice, LIME can be used with a wide range of machine learning models and data types, and can provide valuable insights into how these models are making their predictions.

Pros and Cons:

Pros:

- Local interpretability: LIME provides instance-specific explanations, making it possible to understand how a model is making its predictions on a case-by-case basis.

- Model-agnostic: LIME can be used with a wide range of machine learning models, including black box models that are difficult to interpret using other methods.

- Flexible: LIME can be used with a variety of data types, including text, images, and tabular data.

- Intuitive: LIME generates explanations that are easy to understand, even for non-experts.

- Open-source: LIME is an open-source library that is freely available and can be customized and extended as needed.

Cons:

- Limited to local explanations: LIME is designed to generate instance-specific explanations and may not be suitable for understanding global patterns or trends in the data.

- Sample-based: LIME generates explanations by training an interpretable model on a sample of instances that are similar to the instance being explained. This means that the quality of the explanations may depend on the quality and representativeness of the training data.

- Requires domain knowledge: To use LIME effectively, it is important to have a good understanding of the data and the machine learning model being explained. This may require some domain-specific expertise.

- Computationally intensive: Generating LIME explanations can be computationally intensive, especially for large datasets or complex models. This may limit its usefulness in some applications.

- Not always consistent: Since LIME explanations are based on a sample of instances, they may not be consistent across different samples or runs. This can make it difficult to compare and analyze different explanations.

INTERPRETML

InterpretML is an open-source Python library for interpreting and explaining machine learning models. It provides a range of tools and techniques for understanding how a model is making its predictions, including global feature importance, local explanations, and counterfactual reasoning. The library is designed to be model-agnostic and can be used with a wide range of machine learning models, including regression, classification, and time series models.

InterpretML provides a range of interpretability techniques, including:

- **Feature importance**: Provides tools for understanding the relative importance of different features in a model, both globally and locally.

- **Local explanations**: It provides tools for generating instance-specific explanations that can help to understand why a particular prediction was made.

- **Counterfactual explanations**: Provides tools for generating counterfactual explanations, which show how changing a feature value would affect the model's prediction.

- **Partial dependence plots**: InterpretML provides tools for generating partial dependence plots, which show how changing the value of a feature affects the model's prediction, while controlling for the values of other features.

InterpretML can be used for a variety of tasks, including:

- **Model debugging**: It can help to identify and diagnose problems with a model, such as bias or overfitting.

- **Model selection**: Can be used to compare and evaluate different machine learning models based on their interpretability and performance.

- **Model deployment**: InterpretML can help to explain and justify the decisions made by a machine learning model to stakeholders and regulators.

It is a powerful tool for understanding and interpreting machine learning models, and can be used to improve model transparency, accountability, and trustworthiness.

An example code usage of InterpretML to generate global feature importances and local explanations for a binary classification model:

```
# Import the necessary libraries
from interpret.glassbox import
ExplainableBoostingClassifier
from interpret import show

# Load the dataset
from sklearn.datasets import load_breast_cancer
data = load_breast_cancer()
X, y = data.data, data.target
```

```
# Train an ExplainableBoostingClassifier model
ebm =
ExplainableBoostingClassifier(random_state=42)
ebm.fit(X, y)

# Generate global feature importances
global_explanation = ebm.explain_global()
show(global_explanation)

# Generate local explanations for a specific
instance
local_explanation = ebm.explain_local(X[:5])
show(local_explanation)
```

In this example, we first load the breast cancer dataset from scikit-learn, and split it into features (X) and targets (y). Then, we train an ExplainableBoostingClassifier model on the dataset, and use InterpretML to generate global feature importances and local explanations.

The **explain_global()** method generates global feature importances for the model, which can help to identify the most important features for making predictions. The **show()** method is used to visualize the results.

The **explain_local()** method generates local explanations for a specific instance (in this case, the first 5 instances in the dataset). Local explanations help to understand why a particular prediction was made for a specific instance, and can be useful for debugging and model refinement.

Overall, this example demonstrates how InterpretML can be used to understand and interpret machine learning models, and generate insights that can be used to improve model performance and transparency.

89

Pros and Cons

Pros:

- Model-agnostic: InterpretML can be used with a wide range of machine learning models, making it highly flexible and adaptable to different use cases.

- Interpretable: InterpretML provides a range of tools and techniques for understanding how a model is making its predictions, including global feature importance, local explanations, and counterfactual reasoning.

- Comprehensive: InterpretML provides a range of interpretability techniques, including feature importance, local explanations, counterfactual explanations, and partial dependence plots.

- Easy to use: InterpretML is designed to be easy to use, with a simple and intuitive API.

- Open-source: InterpretML is an open-source library, meaning it is free to use and can be modified and extended by the community.

Cons:

- Limited scalability: InterpretML may be computationally expensive and slow when working with large datasets or complex models.

- Limited support for deep learning: InterpretML is primarily designed for interpretable machine learning models, and may not be well-suited to deep learning models that are inherently less interpretable.

- Limited support for some use cases: While InterpretML provides a wide range of interpretability techniques, there may be some use cases where more specialized techniques are needed.

> INTERPRETML

TEXT PROCESSING

Text processing is analyzing and manipulating textual data to extract useful information or insights. It involves various techniques and tools, including natural language processing (NLP), machine learning, and statistical analysis.

It can be used for various tasks, including text classification, sentiment analysis, entity recognition, topic modeling, and information retrieval. It is used in many industries, including healthcare, finance, and e-commerce, to analyze large volumes of textual data and gain insights into customer behavior, market trends, and other vital factors. It typically involves several steps, including data cleaning and preprocessing, feature extraction, model training and validation, and model deployment. NLP techniques, such as tokenization, part-of-speech tagging, and named entity recognition, are often used to preprocess the data and extract features.

ML algorithms, such as decision trees, support vector machines, and neural networks, are often used to build models that can classify, cluster, or analyze textual data. Statistical analysis techniques, such as regression and clustering, can also be used to gain insights into the data.

Text processing is a rapidly evolving field, with new tools and techniques being developed all the time. It is an important area of research and development as the amount of textual data being generated grows exponentially.

SPACY

Spacy is an open-source library for advanced natural language processing (NLP) in Python. It provides a wide range of NLP capabilities, including tokenization, part-of-speech tagging, named entity recognition, dependency parsing, and more. Spacy is designed to be fast, efficient, and user-friendly, making it a popular choice for developing NLP applications.

It also includes pre-trained models for several languages, making starting with NLP tasks in different languages quick. Additionally, Spacy allows users to train their models on custom datasets, allowing them to create NLP solutions tailored to their specific needs.

Overall, Spacy is a powerful tool for NLP tasks in Python, offering a range of features and pre-trained models to streamline NLP development.

An example of how to use Spacy to extract named entities:

```python
import spacy

# Load a pre-trained model
nlp = spacy.load('en_core_web_sm')

# Text to process
text = "Apple is looking at buying U.K. startup for $1 billion"

# Process the text with the loaded model
doc = nlp(text)
```

```
# Print each token with its part-of-speech
(POS) tag and named entity recognition (NER)
label
for token in doc:
    print(token.text, token.pos_,
token.ent_type_)
```

This code uses the SpaCy library to load a pre-trained English language model (**en_core_web_sm**) and process a text string. It then loops through each token in the processed document and prints out its text, part-of-speech (POS) tag, and named entity recognition (NER) label. The output might look like this:

```
Apple PROPN ORG
is AUX
looking VERB
at ADP
buying VERB
U.K. GPE
startup NOUN
for ADP
$ NUM
1 NUM
billion NUM
```

Pros and Cons

Pros:

- Highly optimized for speed and memory usage, making it efficient even on large datasets.

- Provides state-of-the-art performance in a variety of NLP tasks, including named entity recognition, part-of-speech tagging, dependency parsing, and more.

- Offers easy integration with other Python libraries and frameworks, such as scikit-learn, PyTorch, and TensorFlow.

- Provides a user-friendly and consistent API for performing NLP tasks.

- Includes pre-trained models for multiple languages, making it easier to get started with NLP for non-English languages.

- Has an active development community and good documentation.

Cons:

- Has a steeper learning curve compared to some other NLP libraries.

- May not perform as well on some specific NLP tasks as compared to other libraries that specialize in those tasks.

- While the core library is open source, some of the pre-trained models are only available under commercial licenses.

NLTK

NLTK stands for Natural Language Toolkit. It is a popular open-source library for natural language processing (NLP) tasks in Python. It provides a wide range of functionalities for processing human language such as tokenization, stemming, lemmatization, POS tagging, and more. It also includes a number of pre-built corpora and resources for training machine learning models for NLP tasks. NLTK is widely used for various applications such as text classification, sentiment analysis, machine translation, and information extraction.

A simple example code usage of Python NLTK for tokenization:

```python
import nltk
from nltk.tokenize import word_tokenize

# sample text
text = "This is an example sentence for tokenization."

# tokenize the text
tokens = word_tokenize(text)

# print the tokens
print(tokens)
```

Output:

```
['This', 'is', 'an', 'example', 'sentence', 'for', 'tokenization', '.']
```

97

Pros and Cons

Pros:

- Provides a wide range of natural language processing tools and modules, including tokenization, stemming, tagging, parsing, and classification.

- Has a large community of users and developers, making it easy to find help and resources online.

- Offers support for multiple languages.

- Comes with a variety of datasets and corpora for training and testing models.

- Provides a user-friendly interface for beginners.

- Can be integrated with other Python libraries such as NumPy and Pandas.

Cons:

- Can be slower than other natural language processing libraries due to its reliance on Python data structures.

- The documentation can be overwhelming and difficult to navigate for beginners.

- Some of the algorithms and models may not be as advanced or accurate as those found in other libraries.

- NLTK may not be suitable for large-scale natural language processing tasks due to memory constraints.

- The code can be more verbose and difficult to read compared to other natural language processing libraries.

TEXTBLOB

Python TextBlob is a popular open-source Python library used for processing textual data. It provides a simple API for natural language processing tasks like sentiment analysis, part-of-speech tagging, noun phrase extraction, and more. It is built on top of the Natural Language Toolkit (NLTK) library and provides an easy-to-use interface for text processing.

An example code usage of Python TextBlob:

```python
from textblob import TextBlob

# Creating a TextBlob object
text = "I am really enjoying this course on
natural language processing."
blob = TextBlob(text)

# Sentiment Analysis
sentiment_polarity = blob.sentiment.polarity
sentiment_subjectivity =
blob.sentiment.subjectivity
print("Sentiment Polarity:",
sentiment_polarity)
print("Sentiment Subjectivity:",
sentiment_subjectivity)

# Parts of Speech Tagging
pos_tags = blob.tags
print("Parts of Speech Tags:", pos_tags)

# Named Entity Recognition
ner_tags = blob.noun_phrases
print("Named Entity Recognition:", ner_tags)

# Text Translation
translation = blob.translate(to='fr')
print("Translation to French:", translation)
```

This code performs sentiment analysis, parts of speech tagging, named entity recognition, and text translation using TextBlob. The output will vary depending on the input text used.

Pros and Cons

Pros:

- TextBlob is easy to use and has a simple syntax that makes it accessible to beginners in natural language processing.

- It has built-in sentiment analysis capabilities, which is useful for tasks like social media monitoring and opinion mining.

- TextBlob also includes other natural language processing tasks such as noun phrase extraction, part-of-speech tagging, and classification.

- The library is built on top of the NLTK library, so it has access to the wide range of tools and resources available in NLTK.

Cons:

- TextBlob is not as powerful or customizable as other natural language processing libraries such as spaCy.

- The library may not be as efficient or scalable as other options, especially for large datasets.

- TextBlob's built-in sentiment analysis may not always be accurate, especially for more complex and nuanced text.

Overall, TextBlob is a useful tool for beginners and for simple natural language processing tasks, but it may not be the best choice for more complex or large-scale projects.

CORENLP

Python CoreNLP is a Python wrapper for Stanford CoreNLP, a Java-based natural language processing toolkit developed by Stanford University. It provides a set of tools for various natural language processing tasks such as part-of-speech tagging, named entity recognition, dependency parsing, sentiment analysis, and more. It can be used to analyze and extract information from text data in different formats like plain text, HTML, and XML.

An example code that uses Python CoreNLP to parse a sentence and extract the named entities:

```python
from stanfordcorenlp import StanfordCoreNLP

nlp = StanfordCoreNLP(r'/path/to/corenlp',
memory='8g')

sentence = "John works at Google in
California."
output = nlp.annotate(sentence, properties={
                    'annotators': 'ner',
                    'outputFormat': 'json',
                    'timeout': 1000,
                })
for entity in
output['sentences'][0]['entitymentions']:
    print(entity['text'], entity['ner'])
```

Output:

```
John PERSON
Google ORGANIZATION
California STATE_OR_PROVINCE
```

In this example, we first import the **StanfordCoreNLP** class from the **stanfordcorenlp** package. Then, we create a

103

StanfordCoreNLP object and specify the path to the CoreNLP installation and the amount of memory to be used.

We then define a sentence and use the **annotate()** method of the **StanfordCoreNLP** object to parse the sentence and extract the named entities. We specify the 'ner' annotator to perform named entity recognition and set the output format to 'json'. We also set a timeout of 1000 milliseconds.

Finally, we loop through the named entities in the output and print their text and NER tag

Pros and Cons

Pros:

- CoreNLP provides a wide range of NLP tasks such as part-of-speech tagging, named entity recognition, sentiment analysis, and dependency parsing.

- It is written in Java and can be easily integrated with Python and other programming languages.

- It can handle large text datasets and provide accurate and reliable results.

- It also supports various languages other than English such as Chinese, Spanish, French, German, and Arabic.

Cons:

- The installation and setup process of CoreNLP can be complex and time-consuming.

- CoreNLP requires a significant amount of memory and computational resources to perform tasks on large datasets, which may not be feasible on low-end machines.

- CoreNLP's output may not always be perfect and may require some manual intervention to improve the results.

- It may not be suitable for real-time or online applications due to its high computational requirements.

GENSIM

Gensim is an open-source library for unsupervised topic modeling and natural language processing. It provides a suite of algorithms and models for tasks such as document similarity analysis, document clustering, and topic modeling. The library is designed to be scalable and efficient, with support for streaming data and distributed computing.

It is built on top of NumPy, SciPy, and other scientific computing libraries and provides a simple and intuitive interface for text analysis tasks. It supports a variety of file formats for input data, including plain text, HTML, and XML, and provides built-in support for common text preprocessing steps such as tokenization, stemming, and stopword removal.

Overall, Gensim is a powerful tool for exploring and analyzing large collections of text data, and can be used for a wide range of applications, including information retrieval, recommendation systems, and content analysis.

An example code that uses Gensim to create a simple topic model from a sample text dataset:

```
import gensim
from gensim import corpora
from pprint import pprint

# Define the dataset
data = [
    "I like to eat broccoli and bananas.",
    "I ate a banana and spinach smoothie for
breakfast.",
```

```
    "Chinchillas and kittens are cute.",
    "My sister adopted a kitten yesterday.",
    "Look at this cute hamster munching on a
piece of broccoli."
]

# Tokenize the dataset
tokenized_data =
[gensim.utils.simple_preprocess(text) for text
in data]

# Create a dictionary from the tokenized data
dictionary = corpora.Dictionary(tokenized_data)

# Create a corpus from the dictionary and
tokenized data
corpus = [dictionary.doc2bow(text) for text in
tokenized_data]

# Train the LDA model
lda_model = gensim.models.ldamodel.LdaModel(
    corpus=corpus,
    id2word=dictionary,
    num_topics=2,
    random_state=100,
    update_every=1,
    chunksize=10,
    passes=10,
    alpha='auto',
    per_word_topics=True
)

# Print the topics
pprint(lda_model.print_topics())


Output:

[(0,
  '0.082*"and" + 0.082*"broccoli" + 0.082*"eat"
+ 0.082*"to" + 0.082*"bananas" + 0.060*"i" +
```

```
0.057*"a" + 0.035*"for" + 0.035*"breakfast" +
0.035*"smoothie"'),
 (1,
  '0.077*"kitten" + 0.056*"and" + 0.056*"are" +
0.056*"chinchillas" + 0.056*"cute" + 0.056*"my"
+ 0.056*"sister" + 0.056*"adopted" +
0.056*"yesterday" + 0.056*"look"')]
```

In this example, we use Gensim to tokenize the sample dataset, create a dictionary and corpus, and train an LDA topic model with 2 topics. The output shows the top words associated with each topic.

Pros and Cons

Pros:

- Easy to use API for creating and training topic models

- Supports multiple algorithms for topic modeling, such as Latent Dirichlet Allocation (LDA) and Latent Semantic Analysis (LSA)

- Can handle large datasets efficiently

- Provides tools for text preprocessing, such as tokenization and stopword removal

- Can generate word embeddings using popular algorithms like Word2Vec and FastText

Cons:

- Limited support for deep learning-based techniques compared to other libraries like TensorFlow or PyTorch

- May require some knowledge of statistical inference and machine learning concepts for effective use

- Some functionality may be slower than other libraries due to its focus on memory efficiency and scalability

REGEX

Python Regex (Regular Expression) library is a powerful tool used for pattern matching and text processing. It provides a set of functions and meta-characters that allow us to search and manipulate strings using complex patterns. The regular expression is a sequence of characters that define a search pattern. Python's built-in **re** module provides support for regular expressions in Python. It is a widely used library for performing various text manipulation tasks such as string matching, searching, parsing, and replacing.

An example of using Python's regex library **re** to extract information from a complex string:

```python
import re

# Example string to search through
text = "My phone number is (123) 456-7890 and
my email is example@example.com."

# Define regex patterns to search for
phone_pattern = re.compile(r'\(\d{3}\)\s\d{3}-
\d{4}')  # Matches phone numbers in (123) 456-
7890 format
email_pattern = re.compile(r'\b[\w.-
]+?@\w+?\.\w+?\b')  # Matches email addresses

# Search for matches in the text
phone_match = phone_pattern.search(text)
email_match = email_pattern.search(text)

# Print out the results
if phone_match:
    print("Phone number found:",
phone_match.group())
```

110

```
else:
    print("Phone number not found.")

if email_match:
    print("Email found:", email_match.group())
else:
    print("Email not found.")
```

Output:

```
Phone number found: (123) 456-7890
Email found: example@example.com
```

In this example, we use regular expressions to define patterns to search for a phone number and an email address in a complex string. The patterns are compiled using the **re.compile()** function, and then searched for using the **search()** function. The **group()** function is used to retrieve the actual matched text.

Pros and Cons

Pros:

- Powerful: Regular expressions are a powerful way to search and manipulate text.

- Efficient: The Python Regex library is optimized for performance and can handle large amounts of text quickly.

- Versatile: Regular expressions can be used for a wide range of tasks, from simple string matching to complex text parsing and manipulation.

111

- Flexible: The Python Regex library allows for a great deal of customization, allowing you to create complex patterns and match specific patterns in text.

Cons:

- Steep learning curve: Regular expressions can be difficult to learn, particularly for those new to programming.

- Easy to misuse: Because of their complexity, regular expressions can be prone to errors and can be difficult to debug.

- Limited functionality: While the Python Regex library is powerful, it has some limitations and may not be suitable for all text processing tasks.

- Less readable: Regular expressions can be less readable than other forms of text processing code, making it more difficult to maintain and update code.

IMAGE PROCESSING

Image processing analyzes and manipulates digital images to extract useful information or improve their quality. It involves various techniques and tools, including computer vision, machine learning, and signal processing.

Image processing can be used for a variety of tasks, including object detection and recognition, image segmentation, image enhancement, and pattern recognition. It is used in many industries, including healthcare, manufacturing, and entertainment, to analyze and manipulate digital images and gain insights into the underlying data.

Image processing typically involves several steps, including image acquisition, preprocessing, feature extraction, model training and validation, and model deployment. Computer vision techniques, such as edge detection, object recognition, and image segmentation, are often used to preprocess the data and extract features.

Machine learning algorithms, such as convolutional neural networks (CNNs), are often used to build models that can classify, detect, or analyze digital images. In addition, signal processing techniques, such as filtering and Fourier analysis, can also be used to enhance the quality of digital images.

Image processing is a rapidly evolving field, with new tools and techniques being developed all the time. It is an essential area of research and development as the use of digital images continues to grow in many fields.

OPENCV

OpenCV (Open-Source Computer Vision Library) is a library of programming functions mainly aimed at real-time computer vision. It provides many useful and powerful algorithms and techniques for computer vision and machine learning applications, including image and video processing, object detection and recognition, camera calibration, and more.

OpenCV is written in C++ and provides bindings for Python, making it easy to use in Python applications. It also includes a graphical user interface (GUI) for image and video processing, making it easy to visualize and interact with the data.

Some of the key features of OpenCV include:

- **Image and video processing**: Provides many functions for basic and advanced image and video processing, including filtering, feature detection, image segmentation, and more.

- **Object detection and recognition**: OpenCV provides several methods for object detection and recognition, including Haar cascades, HOG (Histogram of Oriented Gradients), and deep learning-based approaches.

- **Camera calibration**: Includes functions for calibrating cameras, including estimating intrinsic and extrinsic parameters, distortion correction, and more.

- **Machine learning**: Provides several machine learning algorithms for classification, regression, clustering, and more.

Overall, OpenCV is a powerful tool for computer vision and machine learning applications, and is widely used in both academic and industrial settings.

An example code that uses OpenCV to capture video from a webcam and display it on the screen:

```
import cv2

# Create a VideoCapture object
cap = cv2.VideoCapture(0)

while True:
    # Read a frame from the camera
    ret, frame = cap.read()

    # Display the frame
    cv2.imshow('frame', frame)

    # Exit if the 'q' key is pressed
    if cv2.waitKey(1) & 0xFF == ord('q'):
        break

# Release the VideoCapture object and close the
window
cap.release()
cv2.destroyAllWindows()
```

In this code, we first import the **cv2** module, which provides the functions and classes needed to work with OpenCV. We then create a **VideoCapture** object to capture video from the default webcam (device index 0).

115

Inside the **while** loop, we use the **cap.read()** method to read a frame from the camera. The **ret** variable indicates whether the read operation was successful, and the **frame** variable contains the image data for the current frame.

We then use the **cv2.imshow()** function to display the frame on the screen. The first argument to this function is a window name (which can be anything), and the second argument is the image data.

Finally, we use the **cv2.waitKey()** function to wait for a key press. If the 'q' key is pressed, we break out of the loop and release the **VideoCapture** object and close the window.

Pros and Cons

Pros:

- OpenCV is an open source library, which means that it is free to use and modify.

- It has a large community of developers, which ensures that the library is constantly improving and new features are being added.

- OpenCV supports multiple programming languages, including Python, C++, and Java.

- It has a wide range of image and video processing functions, making it a versatile tool for various applications.

- It supports multiple platforms, including Windows, Linux, and MacOS.

Cons:

- OpenCV can have a steep learning curve for beginners due to its large number of functions and complex APIs.

- It requires some knowledge of computer vision and image processing techniques to use effectively.

- The performance of OpenCV can be slow on some devices, especially if running complex algorithms.

- It may not be the best choice for applications that require real-time processing of large amounts of data due to its high computational requirements.

SCIKIT-IMAGE

Python scikit-image is an open-source image processing library that provides algorithms for image processing and computer vision tasks such as filtering, segmentation, object detection, and more. It is built on top of the scientific Python ecosystem, including NumPy, SciPy, and matplotlib.

It is designed to be easy to use and provides a simple and intuitive interface to quickly implement image processing tasks. It supports a variety of image formats and is compatible with Python 3.x.

Some of the key features of scikit-image include:

- **A collection of algorithms for image processing and computer vision**

- **Support for different image formats, including JPEG, PNG, BMP, TIFF, and others**

- **A simple and intuitive API for easy integration with other Python libraries**

- **Compatible with NumPy and SciPy for scientific computing tasks**

- **Comprehensive documentation and examples**

Overall, scikit-image is a powerful tool for image processing and computer vision tasks in Python.

An example code usage of Python scikit-image for image processing:

```python
from skimage import io, filters

# Load image
image = io.imread('example.jpg', as_gray=True)

# Apply Gaussian blur
image_blur = filters.gaussian(image, sigma=1)

# Apply Sobel filter
sobel = filters.sobel(image)

# Display the images
io.imshow_collection([image, image_blur,
sobel])
io.show()
```

In this example, we load an image using the **io.imread** function and apply a Gaussian blur to the image using the **filters.gaussian** function with a **sigma** value of 1. We then apply a Sobel filter to the image using the **filters.sobel** function. Finally, we use the **io.imshow_collection** function to display the original image, the blurred image, and the Sobel-filtered image.

Note that **as_gray=True** is used to convert the image to grayscale. Also, the **io.show()** function is used to display the images.

119

Pros and Cons

Pros:

- scikit-image is a powerful image processing library that provides a wide range of functions for manipulating and analyzing images.

- It is built on top of the popular scientific Python libraries NumPy and SciPy, making it easy to integrate with other scientific computing tools.

- scikit-image has an extensive documentation and an active community, which means that finding help and support is relatively easy.

- The library is open source and freely available under a permissive license, making it accessible to anyone.

Cons:

- Some of the more advanced features of scikit-image can be challenging to use and require a solid understanding of image processing concepts.

- The library may not be as performant as other image processing libraries such as OpenCV for certain tasks.

- Some users have reported issues with installation and compatibility with certain versions of Python and other dependencies.

- scikit-image does not support 3D image processing out of the box, which can be a limitation for some applications.

PILLOW

Pillow is a popular Python library used for image processing tasks. It is a fork of the Python Imaging Library (PIL) and supports many of its features, while also including additional functionality and bug fixes. Pillow provides a comprehensive set of functions for opening, manipulating, and saving image files in a wide variety of formats, including BMP, PNG, JPEG, TIFF, and GIF.

Some of the key features of Pillow include support for various image formats, image enhancement and manipulation functions, drawing and text rendering functions, and support for basic image filtering and transformation operations. It also includes various image processing algorithms such as edge detection, contour detection, and image segmentation.

Pillow is widely used in a variety of image processing applications, including computer vision, machine learning, and web development. It is known for its ease of use, as well as its flexibility and scalability. Additionally, Pillow is open-source software, which means that it is freely available for use and modification by anyone.

Overall, Pillow is a powerful and versatile library for working with image data in Python, and it is an essential tool for anyone working with images in their Python projects.

An example code usage of Pillow using filters:

```python
from PIL import Image, ImageFilter

# Open the image
img = Image.open('image.jpg')

# Apply a Gaussian blur filter
blurred_img =
img.filter(ImageFilter.GaussianBlur(radius=10))

# Apply a sharpen filter
sharpened_img = img.filter(ImageFilter.SHARPEN)

# Display the original image and the filtered
images
img.show()
blurred_img.show()
sharpened_img.show()
```

In this example, we opened an image and applied two different filters to it using Pillow. First, we applied a Gaussian blur filter with a radius of 10 pixels, which creates a blurred effect on the image. Then, we applied a sharpen filter to the original image, which enhances the edges and details in the image. Finally, we displayed all three images (original, blurred, and sharpened) using the **show()** method.

Pros and Cons

Pros:

- Pillow is a well-documented and easy-to-use library for handling images in Python.

- It supports a wide variety of image formats and allows for a range of image manipulation tasks, including cropping, resizing, and filtering.

- Pillow has strong community support and is actively maintained, with frequent updates and bug fixes.

- Pillow is compatible with both Python 2 and 3, making it a versatile choice for image processing in Python.

Cons:

- While Pillow is a powerful library, it may not be suitable for very advanced image processing tasks that require more specialized tools or algorithms.

- Pillow can be relatively slow when processing large or complex images, particularly when compared to more optimized libraries written in lower-level languages like C or C++.

- Pillow may have limited support for some less common image formats, which could be an issue for certain use cases.

MAHOTAS

Python Mahotas is an image processing library that provides a set of algorithms for image processing and computer vision tasks. It is built on top of numpy and scipy and provides functions to perform operations like filtering, segmentation, feature extraction, morphology, and other image processing tasks.

It is designed to work with numpy arrays, making it easy to integrate with other image processing libraries like OpenCV and scikit-image. It provides a fast and efficient implementation of many common image processing algorithms and supports multi-dimensional arrays, making it suitable for working with volumetric data.

Some of the features of Mahotas include:

- **Image filtering and segmentation**

- **Feature extraction and object recognition**

- **Morphological operations like erosion and dilation**

- **Thresholding and edge detection**

- **Watershed segmentation**

- **Region properties and labeling**

An example code usage:

125

```python
import mahotas as mh
import numpy as np
from skimage import data

# Load example image
image = data.coins()

# Convert image to grayscale
image = mh.colors.rgb2gray(image)

# Apply thresholding
thresh = mh.thresholding.otsu(image)

# Label regions
labeled, nr_objects = mh.label(image > thresh)

# Calculate region properties
regions = mh.regionprops(labeled,
intensity_image=image)

# Display results
print("Number of objects:", nr_objects)
for region in regions:
    print("Object:", region.label)
    print("Area:", region.area)
    print("Perimeter:", region.perimeter)
    print("Eccentricity:", region.eccentricity)
    print("Intensity mean:",
region.mean_intensity)
    print("")
```

This code loads an example image, converts it to grayscale, applies Otsu's thresholding method to separate the foreground and background pixels, labels the connected components in the resulting binary image, and calculates various region properties for each object. The output displays the number of objects found and their properties.

126

Pros and Cons

Pros:

- Mahotas provides a range of powerful image processing and feature extraction functions, making it suitable for a variety of computer vision tasks.

- The library is well-documented and provides a range of examples to get started with.

- Mahotas is designed to work efficiently with large image datasets, allowing users to quickly process and analyze large volumes of image data.

- Mahotas is easy to install and use, with a simple API that is easy to understand.

Cons:

- Mahotas does not provide as many features or advanced capabilities as some of the more established computer vision libraries like OpenCV or scikit-image.

- Some of the functions provided by Mahotas can be slow and may not perform as well as other libraries on certain tasks.

- While Mahotas has a relatively active user community, it may not be as widely used or supported as other image processing libraries.

SIMPLEITK

SimpleITK is a high-level interface to the Insight Segmentation and Registration Toolkit (ITK). It is a Python library used for image processing, analysis, and computer vision tasks. SimpleITK allows for easy manipulation of images, such as filtering, segmentation, registration, and feature extraction.

Some common tasks that can be accomplished with SimpleITK include image alignment, registration of multiple images, segmentation of regions of interest, and analysis of image features. The library also provides access to many image analysis algorithms and methods, such as edge detection, object detection, and classification.

SimpleITK is a popular library for medical image processing and analysis, as it provides tools for the analysis of medical images such as CT, MRI, and ultrasound images. It is widely used in the healthcare industry and in research.

Overall, SimpleITK provides a user-friendly interface to the ITK toolkit, making it easier for users to perform complex image processing and analysis tasks. It also has a wide range of applications in various fields, including medical imaging, computer vision, and machine learning.

An example code usage of Python SimpleITK:

```python
import SimpleITK as sitk

# Read an image
image = sitk.ReadImage("image.nii")

# Get the image size
```

```
size = image.GetSize()

# Get the image origin
origin = image.GetOrigin()

# Get the image spacing
spacing = image.GetSpacing()

# Get the image direction
direction = image.GetDirection()

# Print the image information
print("Size:", size)
print("Origin:", origin)
print("Spacing:", spacing)
print("Direction:", direction)

# Display the image
sitk.Show(image)
```

This code reads an image in the NIfTI format using SimpleITK, gets the image size, origin, spacing, and direction, and then displays the image using the **sitk.Show()** function.

Pros and Cons

Pros:

- SimpleITK is a powerful library for image processing and analysis, with a wide range of features for 2D, 3D and higher-dimensional images.

- It provides a simple and intuitive API for performing various tasks, such as reading and writing image files, applying image filters, and segmenting images.

- SimpleITK is built on top of ITK (Insight Segmentation and Registration Toolkit), which is a well-established and widely used image analysis library in the research community.

- SimpleITK can be used with various programming languages, including Python, C++, Java, and Tcl.

Cons:

- SimpleITK has a steeper learning curve compared to some other Python image processing libraries, due to its more complex API and the fact that it is built on top of ITK.

- SimpleITK may not be suitable for all types of image analysis tasks, as it is primarily designed for medical image analysis.

- Some of the more advanced features of SimpleITK, such as registration and segmentation, require a good understanding of the underlying concepts and algorithms.

- SimpleITK can be slower compared to some other Python image processing libraries, due to its more complex algorithms and data structures.

WEB FRAMEWORK

A web framework is a software framework designed to simplify the development of web applications by providing a set of reusable components and tools for building and managing web-based projects. It provides a standardized way to build and deploy web applications by providing a structure, libraries, and pre-written code to handle everyday tasks such as request handling, routing, form processing, data validation, and database access.

Web frameworks typically include programming tools and libraries, such as templates, middleware, and routing mechanisms, that enable developers to write clean, maintainable, and scalable code for web-based projects. In addition, they abstract away much of the low-level details of web development, allowing developers to focus on the high-level functionality of their applications.

There are many web frameworks available in various programming languages, including Python (Django, Flask), Ruby on Rails, PHP (Laravel, Symfony), and JavaScript (React, Angular, Vue.js). These frameworks vary in features, performance, ease of use, and community support.

Web frameworks have become essential for web development because they provide a standardized way to build and maintain web applications, making it easier for developers to build complex web-based projects in less time and with fewer errors.

131

FLASK

Flask is a micro web framework written in Python. It is classified as a microframework because it does not require particular tools or libraries. It has no database abstraction layer, form validation, or any other components where pre-existing third-party libraries provide common functions. However, Flask supports extensions that can add application features as if they were implemented in Flask itself. There are extensions for object-relational mappers, form validation, upload handling, various open authentication technologies, and more.

An example code usage of Flask:

```python
from flask import Flask

app = Flask(__name__)

@app.route('/')
def hello():
    return 'Hello, World!'

if __name__ == '__main__':
    app.run()
```

This creates a simple Flask web application that listens for requests on the root URL (**/**) and returns the string **'Hello, World!'** as a response. When you run this code and navigate to **http://localhost:5000/** in your web browser, you should see the message "Hello, World!" displayed on the page.

Pros and Cons

Pros:

- is a lightweight web framework that is easy to set up and use.

- has a simple and intuitive API that makes it easy to develop web applications.

- provides great flexibility when it comes to database integration, allowing developers to use any database they choose.

- The framework is highly customizable, with a large number of third-party extensions available to add functionality to your application.

- has good community support, with a large number of tutorials, resources, and examples available.

Cons:

- is not as powerful as some of the larger web frameworks, such as Django, which may make it less suitable for larger and more complex projects.

- requires developers to make more decisions about how to structure their application, which can make it more challenging for beginners.

- does not provide built-in support for tasks like form validation or user authentication, which can add additional development time for these features.

- As Flask is not an opinionated framework, it requires more configuration and setup, which can be daunting for developers who are not familiar with web development.

- It is not suitable for developing high-performance web applications that require a lot of concurrency, due to its single-threaded nature.

FASTAPI

FastAPI is a modern, fast (high-performance) web framework for building APIs with Python 3.6+ based on standard Python type hints. It is designed to be easy to use and understand, with a focus on developer productivity and code quality.

FastAPI offers a lot of features out-of-the-box, including:

- **Automatic generation of OpenAPI and JSON Schema documentation**

- **Fast, asynchronous support with Starlette**

- **Dependency injection with FastAPI's Dependency Injection system**

- **Data validation with Pydantic**

- **Interactive API documentation with Swagger UI and ReDoc**

- **Built-in support for GraphQL with Graphene**

- **WebSocket support with Flask-Sockets and WebSocket support**

All of these features make it easy to build and maintain high-quality APIs, while minimizing development time and reducing errors

An example code usage of FastAPI to create a simple API endpoint:

```python
from fastapi import FastAPI

app = FastAPI()

@app.get("/")

async def root():

    return {"message": "Hello World"}
```

This creates a FastAPI instance called **app**. Then, using the **@app.get()** decorator, we create a GET endpoint for the root URL path **/** that returns a JSON object with a "message" key and "Hello World" value.

To run the application, we can save this code in a file, for example **main.py**, and then use a command line interface to start the server:

```
$ uvicorn main:app –reload
```

This command starts the server with the **main** module and **app** instance as the application. The **--reload** option will automatically reload the server on code changes.

Once the server is running, we can access the endpoint at **http://localhost:8000/** in a web browser or make a GET request to the URL using a tool like **curl** or a programming language's **requests** library.

Overall, FastAPI provides a simple and intuitive way to create API endpoints and handle HTTP requests and responses.

Pros and Cons

Pros:

- FastAPI is one of the fastest Python web frameworks, with speeds that are comparable to Node.js and Go.

- It has built-in support for async/await syntax, making it easy to write fast, scalable, and responsive APIs.

- FastAPI has excellent documentation, including an interactive API documentation tool that allows developers to test endpoints directly from their browser.

- It has automatic data validation and serialization, which reduces the amount of boilerplate code required to create robust APIs.

- FastAPI has strong type checking and code autocompletion, which helps prevent errors and speeds up development time.

- FastAPI has a large and growing community of contributors, which means there are many plugins, tools, and tutorials available to help developers get started.

Cons:

- FastAPI is a relatively new framework, so there may be some stability and compatibility issues when using it with other libraries and tools.

- It has a steep learning curve, especially for developers who are not familiar with async/await syntax or type hints.

- FastAPI may not be the best choice for small projects, as its performance benefits are most noticeable in large, complex APIs.

- Because FastAPI is built on top of Starlette, a lower-level ASGI framework, developers may need to learn both frameworks to use it effectively.

- FastAPI's strong focus on performance and type checking may not be necessary for all projects, and could lead to over-engineering and increased development time.

DJANGO

Django is a high-level Python web framework that allows for rapid development of secure and maintainable websites. It follows the model-view-controller (MVC) architectural pattern and provides an extensive set of tools and libraries for handling common web development tasks such as URL routing, form validation, and database schema migrations.

Django's design philosophy emphasizes reusability and "pluggability" of components, meaning that individual parts of a Django project can be easily interchanged and customized to fit specific needs. This makes it particularly suitable for complex web applications with many different features and requirements.

One of the key features of Django is its built-in administration interface, which provides a powerful and customizable web-based interface for managing site content and user accounts. Django also includes built-in support for various database backends, including PostgreSQL, MySQL, and SQLite, as well as integration with popular front-end frameworks like React and Angular.

Overall, Django is a popular choice for web developers looking to build scalable and maintainable web applications quickly and efficiently, particularly those working on large and complex projects with many different components and requirements.

An example code usage of creating a simple Django app that displays a "Hello, World!" message:

1. Install Django by running the command **pip install Django** in your command prompt or terminal.

2. Create a new Django project by running the command **django-admin startproject myproject** in your command prompt or terminal. This will create a new directory called **myproject**.

3. Create a new Django app by running the command **python manage.py startapp myapp** in your command prompt or terminal. This will create a new directory called **myapp** inside the **myproject** directory.

4. Open the **views.py** file inside the **myapp** directory and add the following code:

```python
from django.http import HttpResponse

def hello(request):
    return HttpResponse("Hello, World!")
```

5. Open the **urls.py** file inside the **myapp** directory and add the following code:

```python
from django.urls import path
from . import views

urlpatterns = [
    path('hello/', views.hello, name='hello'),
]
```

6. Open the **urls.py** file inside the **myproject** directory and add the following code:

```
from django.contrib import admin
from django.urls import include, path

urlpatterns = [
    path('admin/', admin.site.urls),
    path('myapp/', include('myapp.urls')),
]
```

7. Start the Django server by running the command **python manage.py runserver** in your command prompt or terminal.

8. Open your web browser and go to **http://127.0.0.1:8000/myapp/hello/**. You should see the message "Hello, World!" displayed in your browser.

This is a very basic example of a Django app, but it demonstrates how you can create a simple web page using Python and the Django framework.

Pros and Cons

Pros:

- Django provides a robust framework for building web applications quickly and efficiently.

- It has a large and active community, which means there are plenty of resources and tools available to help developers.

- Django has a built-in admin interface, which makes it easy to manage data and content.

- The framework is secure by default, which helps protect against common web application vulnerabilities.

- Django has excellent documentation and a well-structured architecture that makes it easy to understand and maintain code.

Cons:

- Django is a relatively heavy framework, which means it can be slower and more resource-intensive than some other options.

- The built-in admin interface is powerful, but it may not be customizable enough for some projects.

- Django can have a steep learning curve, particularly for developers who are new to web development or to Python itself.

- The framework's opinionated nature can sometimes be limiting, particularly for developers who prefer more flexibility and control over their code.

DASH

Dash is a web application framework for building interactive web-based dashboards. It is built on top of Flask, Plotly.js, and React.js, which makes it easy to build complex and data-driven web applications. Dash allows users to create interactive dashboards with interactive graphs, tables, and widgets without needing to know HTML, CSS, or JavaScript.

With Dash, you can build dynamic web applications that can handle millions of data points and real-time updates. It has a simple syntax and can be used with any Python data science stack, including NumPy, Pandas, and Scikit-learn. Dash also supports deployment to the cloud using services like Heroku and AWS.

Overall, Dash is a powerful and flexible tool for building data-driven web applications and dashboards that can be used in a variety of domains, including finance, healthcare, and government.

An example code usage of Python Dash:

```python
import dash
import dash_core_components as dcc
import dash_html_components as html

app = dash.Dash()

app.layout = html.Div(children=[
    html.H1(children='Hello Dash'),

    html.Div(children='''
        Dash: A web application framework for
Python.
```

143

```
        '''),

    dcc.Graph(
        id='example-graph',
        figure={
            'data': [
                {'x': [1, 2, 3], 'y': [4, 1,
2], 'type': 'bar', 'name': 'SF'},
                {'x': [1, 2, 3], 'y': [2, 4,
5], 'type': 'bar', 'name': u'Montréal'},
            ],
            'layout': {
                'title': 'Dash Data
Visualization'
            }
        }
    )
])

if __name__ == '__main__':
    app.run_server(debug=True)
```

This code creates a simple Dash application that displays a bar chart. When you run the application, you will see a web page with the title "Hello Dash" and a bar chart that displays two sets of data for the cities of San Francisco and Montreal.

Pros and Cons

Pros:

- Easy to learn and use, especially for those familiar with Python.

- Highly customizable dashboards and visualizations.

144

- Provides interactivity and real-time data updates.

- Can be integrated with other Python libraries and frameworks.

- Supports both local and cloud-based deployment.

Cons:

- Limited styling options for the dashboard and visualizations.

- Can be slower for large-scale applications.

- Requires knowledge of HTML, CSS, and JavaScript for advanced customization.

- Limited support for certain data visualization libraries.

PYRAMID

Pyramid is a web framework designed to make the development of web applications more accessible by providing a simple and flexible approach to building web applications. Pyramid is a lightweight framework that is easy to learn and use. It is based on the WSGI standard and provides many features, including URL routing, templating, authentication, and database integration.

It is designed to be modular and extensible. It provides core features that can be extended with add-ons and third-party libraries. It's also highly configurable, allowing developers to customize the framework's behavior to fit their specific needs.

Pyramid is built on top of the Pylons web framework and incorporates many features. Other popular web frameworks, including Django and Ruby on Rails, also inspire it.

Overall, Pyramid is an excellent choice for building complex web applications requiring high flexibility and customization. Its modularity and extensibility make it easy to adapt to various use cases. At the same time, its core features provide a solid foundation for building robust and scalable web applications.

A simple example of a Pyramid web application:

First, you need to install Pyramid by running **pip install pyramid** in your terminal.

Then, create a new file called **app.py** and add the following code:

```
from wsgiref.simple_server import make_server
from pyramid.config import Configurator
from pyramid.response import Response

def home(request):
    return Response('Hello, Pyramid!')

if __name__ == '__main__':
    with Configurator() as config:
        config.add_route('home', '/')
        config.add_view(home,
route_name='home')
        app = config.make_wsgi_app()
    server = make_server('localhost', 8000,
app)
    print('Server running at
http://localhost:8000')
    server.serve_forever()
```

This code sets up a very basic Pyramid web application with a single route **/** that responds with "Hello, Pyramid!".

To run the application, simply run **python app.py** in your terminal and navigate to **http://localhost:8000** in your web browser. You should see the message "Hello, Pyramid!" displayed in your browser.

Note that this is just a simple example to get you started with Pyramid. There's a lot more you can do with it, such as using templates, working with databases, and more.

Pros and Cons

Pros:

147

- Flexible and easy to use for both small and large-scale web applications.

- Provides a lot of features out of the box, such as URL routing, templating, and authentication.

- Can be used with different databases, such as PostgreSQL, MySQL, SQLite, and Oracle.

- Supports a variety of security features, including cross-site scripting (XSS) prevention, CSRF protection, and secure password hashing.

- Has a large and active community that provides support and updates.

Cons:

- Can have a steeper learning curve compared to other Python web frameworks, especially for beginners.

- Has a more minimalist approach to web development, which may require more manual configuration and setup.

- Can be less suitable for rapid prototyping or small-scale projects, as it requires more effort to set up and configure.

- Documentation can be less comprehensive compared to other Python web frameworks.

WEB SCRAPING

Web scraping is the process of extracting data from websites automatically using software or a script. It involves fetching web pages, parsing the HTML or XML content, and extracting useful information from the web pages, such as text, images, links, and other data.

Web scraping can be used for a variety of purposes, such as data mining, research, price monitoring, and content aggregation. Businesses commonly use it; researchers and data analysts gather data from multiple sources, analyze it, and use it for decision-making.

Web scraping can be done manually, but it is more commonly automated using specialized software or tools known as web scrapers or web crawlers. These tools can be programmed to visit websites, follow links, and extract specific data from web pages in a structured or unstructured format.

Web scraping raises ethical and legal concerns, mainly when extracting data from copyrighted or private websites. In addition, some websites may also have restrictions on web scraping, such as terms of service or robots.txt files, that limit or prohibit web scraping activities. Therefore, it is essential to understand the legal and ethical implications of web scraping and to use it responsibly and ethically.

BEAUTIFULSOUP

BeautifulSoup is a Python library used for web scraping purposes to pull the data out of HTML and XML files. It creates a parse tree from page source code that can be used to extract data in a hierarchical and more readable manner.

BeautifulSoup provides a few simple methods and Pythonic idioms for navigating, searching, and modifying a parse tree. It sits on top of an HTML or XML parser and provides Pythonic idioms for iterating, searching, and modifying the parse tree.

It is a powerful tool for web scraping and can be used for various applications, such as data mining, machine learning, and web automation.

An example code usage of BeautifulSoup:

Suppose we want to scrape the title and the links of the top 5 articles from the homepage of the New York Times.

```python
import requests
from bs4 import BeautifulSoup

url = "https://www.nytimes.com/"
response = requests.get(url)
soup = BeautifulSoup(response.content,
'html.parser')

articles = soup.find_all('article')[:5]

for article in articles:
    title =
article.find('h2').get_text().strip()
    link = article.find('a')['href']
```

```
print(title)
print(link)
print()
```

This code sends a GET request to the New York Times homepage, extracts the HTML content using the BeautifulSoup library, and then finds all of the **article** elements on the page. For each article, it extracts the title and the link and prints them to the console.

Output:

```
New York City Vaccine Mandate Takes Effect for
Private Employers

https://www.nytimes.com/2022/01/20/nyregion/new
-york-city-vaccine-mandate.html

Wall Street Is Bracing for a Reshuffle

https://www.nytimes.com/2022/01/20/business/wal
l-street-banks-q4-earnings.html

Biden Administration Plans to Move Afghans to
Third Countries, but Fewer Will Qualify

https://www.nytimes.com/2022/01/20/us/politics/
afghanistan-refugees.html

E.U. Chief Has a Warning for Russia Over Its
Actions in Ukraine

https://www.nytimes.com/2022/01/20/world/europe
/eu-russia-ukraine.html

Elliott Abrams, Who Oversaw U.S. Policy in
Latin America, Dies at 73
```

151

```
https://www.nytimes.com/2022/01/20/us/politics/
elliott-abrams-dead.html
```

In this example, we use Python's requests library to send an HTTP GET request to the specified URL. We then pass the HTML content of the response to BeautifulSoup, which parses the HTML and creates a parse tree. We use the **find_all()** method to find all the **article** elements on the page and then extract the title and link information from each **article** element using the **find()** method. Finally, we print the title and link information to the console.

Pros and Cons

Pros:

1. Easy to learn: BeautifulSoup is an intuitive library that is easy to learn and use for scraping web pages.

2. Flexible: It can handle all types of HTML and XML files and allows you to work with different parsers.

3. Supports CSS selectors: You can use CSS selectors to find specific HTML elements, which makes it easier to scrape data from web pages.

4. Wide community: BeautifulSoup has a large community of users who regularly contribute to the library and provide support to fellow developers.

Cons:

1. Slow: BeautifulSoup can be slow when working with large web pages or data sets.

2. Limited JavaScript support: It does not support JavaScript rendering, which can be a disadvantage when scraping dynamic web pages.

3. Limited error handling: It does not handle errors or exceptions very well, which can make debugging difficult.

4. No built-in persistence: You will need to use other libraries or tools to store the scraped data, as BeautifulSoup does not have built-in persistence.

SCRAPY

Scrapy is an open-source web crawling framework that is used to extract data from websites. It is built on top of the Twisted framework and provides an easy-to-use API for crawling web pages and extracting information. Scrapy is designed to handle large-scale web crawling tasks and can be used to extract data for a wide range of applications, including data mining, information processing, and even for building intelligent agents.

Scrapy uses a pipeline-based architecture that allows users to write reusable code for processing the scraped data. It also includes built-in support for handling common web protocols like HTTP and HTTPS, as well as for handling asynchronous requests.

In addition to its powerful web crawling capabilities, Scrapy also includes features for data cleaning, filtering, and normalization. This makes it a great tool for extracting structured data from unstructured web pages, which can be difficult to do with other web scraping tools.

It is highly customizable and can be extended with plugins and third-party libraries. Its community is also very active, with a wide range of resources available for users to learn from and get help with any issues they encounter.

Scrapy is a powerful web crawling framework that provides a lot of flexibility and functionality for extracting data from websites. However, it does require some knowledge of Python and web development to use effectively.

An example of how to use Scrapy to scrape quotes from the website http://quotes.toscrape.com/:

First, install Scrapy by running **pip install scrapy** in your command prompt or terminal.

Then, create a new Scrapy project by running **scrapy startproject quotes_scraper** in your command prompt or terminal. This will create a new directory called **quotes_scraper**.

Next, navigate to the **spiders** directory within the **quotes_scraper** directory and create a new file called **quotes_spider.py**. Add the following code to this file:

```python
import scrapy


class QuotesSpider(scrapy.Spider):
    name = "quotes"

    start_urls = [
        'http://quotes.toscrape.com/page/1/',
    ]

    def parse(self, response):
        for quote in response.css('div.quote'):
            yield {
                'text':
quote.css('span.text::text').get(),
                'author': quote.css('span
small::text').get(),
                'tags': quote.css('div.tags
a.tag::text').getall(),
            }

        next_page = response.css('li.next
a::attr(href)').get()
        if next_page is not None:
```

155

```
        yield response.follow(next_page,
self.parse)
```

This spider defines the name of the spider, the starting URL to scrape, and a **parse** method which is responsible for extracting the quotes from each page and following links to the next page if they exist.

To run the spider, navigate to the **quotes_scraper** directory in your command prompt or terminal and run **scrapy crawl quotes**. This will start the spider and output the scraped quotes to your console.

Here is an example of what the output might look like:

```
{'text': '"The world as we have created it is a
process of our thinking. It cannot be changed
without changing our thinking."', 'author':
'Albert Einstein', 'tags': ['change', 'deep-
thoughts', 'thinking', 'world']}
{'text': '"It is our choices, Harry, that show
what we truly are, far more than our
abilities."', 'author': 'J.K. Rowling', 'tags':
['abilities', 'choices']}
{'text': '"There are only two ways to live your
life. One is as though nothing is a miracle.
The other is as though everything is a
miracle."', 'author': 'Albert Einstein',
'tags': ['inspirational', 'life', 'live',
'miracle', 'miracles']}
```

Each quote is represented as a dictionary with keys for the quote text, author, and tags.

Pros and Cons

Pros:

- Powerful web scraping framework that handles asynchronous requests and supports XPath and CSS selectors

- Ability to extract data from a variety of sources such as websites, APIs, and even databases

- Built-in support for handling common web scraping tasks like avoiding bot detection and managing user sessions

- Includes built-in support for exporting scraped data to various formats, including JSON, CSV, and XML

- Supports various customization options, including middleware, extensions, and pipelines

Cons:

- Steep learning curve, especially for beginners who are new to web scraping

- Requires some knowledge of XPath and CSS selectors to extract data from web pages

- Not suitable for all types of web scraping tasks, especially those that require more complex scraping logic or use of machine learning models

- Requires more setup and configuration compared to other simpler web scraping libraries, which can be time-consuming

SELENIUM

Selenium is a library that enables web automation and testing by providing a way to interact with web pages programmatically. It allows developers to automate web browsers, simulate user interactions with websites, and scrape web data.

Selenium is widely used in testing and automation of web applications. It supports various programming languages including Python, Java, C#, Ruby, and JavaScript, and can work with different browsers such as Chrome, Firefox, Safari, and Internet Explorer.

With Selenium, you can create scripts to automate repetitive tasks such as form filling, clicking buttons, navigating through pages, and extracting data from web pages.

Overall, Selenium is a powerful tool for web automation and testing and can greatly simplify tasks that would otherwise be time-consuming and laborious.

An example code usage of Selenium for web scraping:

```python
from selenium import webdriver
from selenium.webdriver.common.by import By

# Set up the driver
driver = webdriver.Chrome('path/to/chromedriver')

# Navigate to the website you want to scrape
driver.get('https://www.example.com')
```

```
# Find the element you want to interact with
and perform actions
element = driver.find_element(By.XPATH,
'//button[@id="button-id"]')
element.click()

# Extract the data you want from the website
data_element = driver.find_element(By.XPATH,
'//div[@class="data-class"]')
data = data_element.text

# Clean up and close the driver
driver.quit()
```

In this example, we're using the Chrome driver and navigating to a website. We then find a button element and click it, which causes some data to load on the page. We then find the element that contains the data we want to scrape and extract its text. Finally, we clean up and close the driver.

Note that web scraping can be a legally and ethically gray area, and some websites may have terms of service that prohibit it. Be sure to check the website's policies and be respectful in your scraping activities.

Pros and Cons

Pros:

- Can interact with web pages as if you were using a web browser, allowing for more complex scraping tasks

- Supports a wide range of browsers including Chrome, Firefox, Safari, and Internet Explorer

- Can handle dynamic content loaded by JavaScript, AJAX, and other technologies

- Supports headless browsing, which allows you to run the scraping tasks without a graphical user interface

- Supports various programming languages including Python, Java, Ruby, and C#

Cons:

- Can be slower than other web scraping libraries due to its reliance on browser automation

- Requires more setup and configuration compared to other libraries

- Can be more resource-intensive, as it requires a browser instance to run

- May not be suitable for all web scraping tasks, particularly those that require high speed and scalability

> SELENIUM

Also available from the Author

A PRIMER TO THE 42 MOST COMMONLY USED MACHINE LEARNING ALGORITHMS
(WITH CODE SAMPLES)

Whether you're a data scientist, software engineer, or simply interested in learning about machine learning, "A Primer to the 42 Most commonly used Machine Learning Algorithms (With Code Samples)" is an excellent resource for gaining a comprehensive understanding of this exciting field.

Available on Amazon:
https://www.amazon.com/dp/B0BT911HDM

Kindle: **(B0BT8LP2YW)**
Paperback: **(ISBN-13: 979-8375226071)**

MINDFUL AI

Reflections on Artificial Intelligence

Inspirational Thoughts & Quotes on Artificial Intelligence
(Including 13 illustrations, articles & essays for the fundamental
understanding of AI)

*The field of AI is highly interdisciplinary & evolutionary.
The more AI penetrates our life and environment, the
more comprehensive the points we have to consider and
adapt. Technological developments are far ahead of
ethical & philosophical interpretations; this fact is
disturbing.*

We need to close this gap as soon as possible.

~ (Mindful AI)

Available on Amazon:
https://www.amazon.com/dp/B0BKMK6HLJ

Kindle: **(ASIN: B0BKLCKM22)**
Paperback: **(ISBN-13: 979-8360396796)–**

INSIDE ALAN TURING:
QUOTES & CONTEMPLATIONS

Alan Turing is generally considered the father of computer science and artificial intelligence. He was also a theoretical biologist who developed algorithms to explain complex patterns using simple inputs and random fluctuation as a side hobby. Unfortunately, his life tragically ended in suicide in 1954, after he was chemically castrated as punishment (instead of prison) for 'criminal' gay acts.

"We can only see a short distance ahead, but we can see plenty there that needs to be done."

~ Alan Turing

Available on Amazon:
https://www.amazon.com/dp/B09K25RTQ6

Kindle: **(ASIN: B09K3669BX)**
Paperback: **(ISBN- 979-8751495848)**

www.ingramcontent.com/pod-product-compliance
Lightning Source LLC
La Vergne TN
LVHW052100060326

832903LV00060B/2444